Ecowomanism at the Panamá Canal

Environment and Religion in Feminist-Womanist, Queer, and Indigenous Perspectives

Series Editor: Gabrie'l Atchison

Environment and Religion in Feminist-Womanist, Queer, and Indigenous Perspectives is a series that explores the subject of ecofeminism from feminist-womanist, queer, and indigenous perspectives. The governing assumption of the series is that ecofeminism is not only a mode of scholarly discourse and analysis, but also a hub for social formation and action. What distinguishes this series in particular is that it focuses on ecofeminism as a disciplinary matrix through which the voices of women, particularly women of color, and indigenous peoples can speak from their religious and spiritual traditions and practices to address the environmental challenges and concerns of the age. Volumes in this series will attend to the environmental and ecological issues that impact women, people of color, and indigenous populations, as these communities are, in almost all respects, the most immediately threatened by contemporary climate and ecological changes and catastrophes. Works in the series will focus on the history; scholarly resources and perspectives; constructive practices; religious, spiritual, and natural traditions from which these voices speak; and how these can provide alternative narratives, illuminate hidden agendas, and generate resistance to environmental and religious racism and exploitation.

Titles in the Series

Ecowomanism at the Panamá Canal

Black Women, Labor, and Environmental Ethics

Sofía Betancourt

LEXINGTON BOOKS

Lanham • Boulder • New York • London

Published by Lexington Books
An imprint of The Rowman & Littlefield Publishing Group, Inc.
4501 Forbes Boulevard, Suite 200, Lanham, Maryland 20706
www.rowman.com

86-90 Paul Street, London EC2A 4NE

British Library Cataloguing in Publication Information Available

Library of Congress Cataloging-in-Publication Data Available

ISBN 978-1-7936-4138-0 (cloth)
ISBN 978-1-7936-4140-3 (pbk.)
ISBN 978-1-7936-4139-7 (electronic)

for the ancestors

Contents

List of Figures

Acknowledgments

A project that stretches over a long period of time requires the support of many. I am profoundly grateful to the ancestors, mentors, colleagues, and loved ones who have been with me on this journey. I am grateful to the remarkable committee members supporting my work: Emilie Townes, Kathryn Lofton, and Edward Rugemer. I am also thankful for those who served as committee members along the way: Katie G. Cannon, Willis Jenkins, and Jennifer Herdt. I am blessed to have brilliant mentors, many of them friends, who have been unshakeable in their support. I am particularly grateful to Devorah Greenstein, Julia Watts Belser, Melanie Harris, Ibrahim Farajajé, Gabriella Lettini, Rebecca Parker, Dan McKanan, Elías Ortega, Rosemary Bray McNatt, Valerie Miles-Tribble, Cynthia Moe-Lobeda, Hazel Carby, and Jennifer Leath. Thank you also to my colleagues at Starr King School for the Ministry who have been positive and patient allies along the way.

Librarians are the unremarked and too-little-celebrated backbone of the academic enterprise. I have had the good fortune to work with remarkable staff at Biblioteca Presidente Roberto F. Chiari in Panamá City, Panamá; the Latin American and Caribbean Collection of the George A. Smathers Libraries at the University of Florida, Gainesville; the Schomburg Center for Research in Black Culture (part of the New York Public Library) in Manhattan; the American Folklife Center at the Library of Congress; the Earl S. Tupper Library in Tropical Biology of the Smithsonian Tropical Research Institute in Panamá City; and the Schmulowitz Collection of Wit and Humor in San Francisco, California. My gratitude in particular extends to Aleyda Aguilar and Margarita Vargas-Betancourt for their kind support of this project.

There are friends and colleagues who have gone above and beyond over the years, many more than can be named in a brief acknowledgment. In particular, I want to remember Chris Long, Adam Robersmith, Cristhal Bennett, Barb Greve, mandi huizenga, Michael Macias, Jaelynn Scott, Mylo Way, Ranwa Hammamy, Taya Shere, Sheri Prud'homme, Megan Dowdell, Ana Lara, Kim Hampton, Kierstin Homblette Allen, Jenny Weil, Janice Marie Johnson, Hope Johnson, Leslie Takahashi, Mitra Rahnema, Alicia Forde, Mykal Slack, Joellynn Monahan, Joanne Braxton, Bill Sinkford, Leon Spencer, Jesse King, Jami Yandle, Black Lives of Unitarian Universalism, Yale's Black Feminist Reading Group, Emerging Unitarian Universalist Scholars Group, Dawn Fortune for the hand-forged blade on my desk, and Alex Kapitan for loving and trusted editing.

I am grateful for the collaborative learning I have experienced with my students over the years, and for tangible support from the Fund for Nurturing Unitarian Universalist Scholarship and the Unitarian Universalist Women's Federation.

Devorah Greenstein, while already mentioned above, served as a primary support for research, editing, stamina, and encouragement over many long years. There are not words enough to express how lucky I am to have her as chosen family. Thank you to my family as a whole; most especially to my parents Patricia Lynton and Octavio Betancourt, my partner Sam Ames, and my chosen family Shannon Eizenga and Devorah Greenstein for loving me all the way through. Thanks to my grandmother Carmen Lynton Holt, whose memories were never recorded but whose histories of "making do" were etched into her countenance.

Lastly and always, my respect and gratitude to the ancestors without whom I would still be staring at a blank page.

Chapter 1

Ecowomanism at the Panamá Canal

The seeds of this project were borne on the winds of a childhood love of nature, a call to herbal healing, a bachelor's degree in what was then called ethnobotany, and departure from the field of ethnobotany in reaction to its embedded settler colonial ideologies and frequent disregard for sustainable environmental practices. Those seeds settled in the fertile soil of Panamá that nurtured me from an early age. Periodically I would return with my mother—or be sent to the arms of my grandparents—to settle back into the humid air, blistering sun, rich soils, and a longing for life that I didn't get to experience day-to-day in the urban centers of the United States. I never failed to notice how the struggling hanging plants and green life advertised as great for apartment living in the United States thrived in gigantic hedges in Panamá, vibrant with life, rather than trapped in the tiny 6-inch terra-cotta pots we had at home. I also grew up hearing stories of how hard my mother's contemporaries worked to raise their children outside of the Caribbean, to provide us with important opportunities, and how they would gather together to laugh about how these same children wanted nothing more than to return to their parents' countries of origin and contribute something. The stories were told tongue in cheek, and with a large amount of pride. I think that is part of what lent me the courage to embark on this topic from a position of generational displacement, with prayers for ancestral support and family forgiveness for any errors I would make. I pray my mother and all of her mothers, too, are laughing.

SCOPE OF THE PROJECT

They came from many places and spoke different languages. Bringing with them nothing but their desire to work and their hopes, they came together to build the engineering feat that still marvels the world. Most came from Barbados, but also from Martinique, Guadeloupe, Trinidad and Jamaica. Spanish, Italians, Greeks, Hindus, Americans, Armenians, Cubans, Costa Ricans, Colombians and Panamanians also contributed to the effort. They managed to understand each other, started families, made fortunes, and exalted the country.[1]

Ecowomanism at the Panamá Canal: Black Women, Labor, and Environmental Ethics constructs a transnational ecowomanist ethic that reclaims inherited environmental cultures across multiple sites of displacement. Rather than beginning with the assumption that full participation in an earth community requires intimate knowledge of the local ecosystem, this inquiry seeks ethical understandings from communities that have been forcibly displaced from their ancestral homes. I develop an ecowomanist moral anthropology that engages questions of dignity, relationality, and environmental justice through extensive archival research and close analysis of oral history fieldwork. This ecowomanist moral anthropology, a theoethical understanding of human nature, and its intrinsic interrelatedness with all of creation draw from the moral wisdom of women in the African diaspora. Most specifically, this work is guided by the experiences of West Indian women, imported to Panamá by the United States from across the Caribbean, whose labor supported the building of the Panamá Canal.

The Panamá Canal represents the largest investment of capital in any enterprise outside of war in human history. Its construction, traditionally hailed as a triumph of American progress over nature, represents the early seeds of the American empire. This project employs postcolonial ecocriticism to construct a contemporary transnational environmental ethics that takes seriously the brutal impact of colonialism and empire on both human and nonhuman nature. While catastrophic notions of the right to human dominion over all of creation have inexcusably and unquestionably debilitated ecosystems across the globe, that rapacious drive for dominion cannot be separated from the desire to control and "civilize" dark-skinned bodies. The conflation of these two domineering worldviews drives the destruction of both natural resources and the fecundity of the land. This text develops an ecowomanist moral anthropology that begins in the environmental cultures, diasporic religious traditions, and moral stories borne across multiple geographic displacements by Panamá Canal laborers to engage environmental ethics on moral ground that is neither colonized nor predefined by Eurocentric legacies of control.

This study undertakes an ecowomanist analysis of the ethical rhetoric surrounding the United States' original construction and subsequent expansion of the Panamá Canal. It begins in the late 1890s when the United States was questioning what some framed as a "right" or even a "duty" to expand its influence internationally through the construction of canals and the annexation of land. It continues through the first expansion of the canal in 1939, and proposes the idea of *ecocreolization* as a conceptual tool in the work of environmental ethics. Ecocreolization is an agential response to the slow violence of neo-imperialism and forced displacement/migration. It is the process of self-definition and meaning making that arises in response to interrelated violence centered on race, class, gender, and the environment. Ecocreolization insists that the formation of African diasporic identities and cultures cannot be fully understood without engaging our relationship to Earth. Through coconstructions of race, gender, and the natural world, ecocreolization reveals what it means to be fully human in a time of climate disruption.

Such analysis calls for the articulation of a comprehensive ecowomanist ethics applicable to environmental devastation beyond the historical impact of the Panamá Canal. This book documents how imperial legacies continue to marginalize and harm both undervalued human populations in the Global South and the environment as a whole. It proposes an ecowomanist moral anthropology, with the reclamation of diasporic practices collectively labeled as *Obeah*, as a site of repair. Through archival research and oral history, *Ecowomanism at the Panamá Canal* retrieves family history and elevates the long-silenced wisdom of women migrants from the Caribbean, seeking to preserve the voices and legacies of those whose hands actually built the canal—the so-called "silver men" and women who faced mud, mosquitoes, and malaria while building a literal pathway to the American empire.

MOTHER WIT MEETS SABIDURÍA IN INTERCULTURAL KNOWLEDGE PRODUCTION

Womanist, mujerista, and Latina feminist ethicists and theologians reshape our ways of knowing by placing Black and Latina women at the center of the theoethical project. With the birth pains expected during the expansion and at times repair that honors the labor of our foremothers, these three epistemological perspectives productively influence one another to the benefit of scholars who utilize a combined approach. Yet most writings in the field maintain a separation between Latinas and Black women, either focusing entirely on those of us living in the United States and thereby on racial and ethnic categories predetermined by the state or overlooking the orgullo (pride and sense of self) that many Black-identified Latinas and Latina Americans hold for our African and Indigenous heritages. Too often the mestizaje and mulatez in Latina or Hispanic cultures—the racial and ethnic mixity that Ada María Isasi-Díaz writes of so powerfully in her work—are seen as an aspect of what makes Latinas *Latina* rather than as an ongoing and knowledge-producing inheritance that needs to be explored in its own right.[2] This project embraces the scholarly work of Latina feminist intercultural theology to identify a diasporic intercultural feminist theoethics whose epistemological assumptions trace the mother wit and sabiduría (wisdom) of women across the range of Afro-Latinx identities. It further builds on the shared histories of struggle, strength, and survival of both Black women and Latinas as critical sites of knowledge production, and organizing to dismantle the immense colonial legacy of climate disruption.

When scholars at the first Inter-American Symposium on Feminist Intercultural Theology came together to develop an intercultural approach to dismantling the oppressive religious and cultural legacies of globalization, their voices called for transnational knowledge production and understanding interculturality as a journey of the in-between.[3] The work of Latina feminist intercultural theology identifies the need to understand Latin America historically as a created geopolitics of knowledge,[4] and that Latin America's interculturality therefore requires the acceptance of plurality and plural truths.[5] It is past time for Latina and Black women to reclaim our own historical perspectives on ways of knowing, and to reject false boundaries of difference put in place to weaken our inherent strengths. This includes the ongoing need for an expansive engagement with dismantling the gender binary and working to expand both womanist and Latina feminist methodologies with a commitment to undermine cissexism and transphobia. A diasporic intercultural feminist theoethics allows the work of environmental ethics to celebrate *true* differences without allowing it to silence shared histories and struggles. It situates our epistemic truths and our moral values in the linked arms of our mothers.

The idea of mothers as vital keepers and teachers of cultural wisdom is shared among Latina feminist and womanist scholars, as is the conviction that key community values can be found not only in our religious practices and daily lived experiences but also in the literary depictions of those same things. Our griots and lore keepers are often our lyricists and our poets. Womanist foremother and ethicist Katie Cannon understood this, and created a foundational womanist methodology for the study of ethics by drawing on Black women's literary writings as a source for moral truth. Cannon identifies women of the African diaspora as the wisdom keepers and teachers of community values. As such, their writings and other artistic expressions are treasure troves for exploring cultural values that might otherwise be overlooked when approaching the study of ethics through the dominant canon.[6] In reclaiming the values of our inherited cultural teachings, Cannon further redeems the silenced voice, restoring a path through stories held and retold by those who loved us most. Theologian Jeanette Rodríguez makes a similar claim when she writes about the epistemology of Mexican American women living in the United States in order to better understand their mestizaje, which for her comprises a type of code-switching between the dominant culture and an individual's Latina ethnicity. She writes:

> This particular Latino/a culture has evolved from a tradition that is often described as *flor y canto* (flower and song). According to this world view, the deepest recesses of being human can only be expressed in the poetry of metaphor and beauty. While it recognizes the significances of reason and logic, this particular world view takes seriously the affect, the intuitive, and the aesthetic.[7]

In order to better employ both Latina feminist and womanist methodologies in intercultural knowledge production, I draw on Rhonda Frederick's understanding of multiple mythographies in the history of West Indian women who migrated to work on the Panamá Canal (see "Methodology").

These women carried within them multiple languages, complex histories, multifaceted cultures, and plural truths. This epistemological undertaking benefits from intercultural methodologies that begin with the assumption that such connections are not only possible but vital. There is a difference between the interconnections of Latina and Black women's religiosity and daily experiences as acts of solidarity and interrelated histories, on the one hand, and the realities of women who live on the supposed dividing lines between the two, on the other. In no way should the perspectives of Afro-Latinx women be seen as the sole space of overlap between womanist and Latina feminist theoethical methodologies. There are many other cultural diversities and gender expressions that must be included in the feminist theoethical work of liberation.

To reclaim moral truths born of generations of creative, rehumanizing struggle requires centering the importance of diaspora within the context of theoethical scholarship. Diasporic intercultural feminist theoethics not only embraces the connections between cultural groups for the benefit of the whole, it also reminds us of the serial migrations and displacements, the ancestral rotations, that allow us to fully value one another. In moving from theology to theoethics, we draw on the work of womanist scholars who remind us that our mothers lived their cultural inheritances, carrying their experiences of the sacred into the world they were building day by day.

EMERGENT ECOWOMANIST ETHICS

The work of rescripting human engagement with the natural world suffers from the histories and legacies of injustice found within human communities.

Throughout the production of scholarship on religious environmental ethics a liberationist strand emphasizes the repercussions of patriarchy, racism, colonialism, resource theft, and neo-imperialistic control of the two-thirds world on the rapid progression of climate disruption. Constructions of environmental ethics of liberation (whether ecowomanist, ecofeminist, ecojustice, postcolonial, or grounded in the language of human rights) seek to unmask and remediate multiple, oppressive hegemonic ideologies of supremacy in order to undermine environmental violence and rebuild the ecological community. This understanding can hopefully serve as a new rootstock for growing moral guidelines to increase the possibility of sustaining life. Questions of agency, moral authority, and accountability remain very much at stake, determining whether hegemonic forces will continue to define our moral living.

Emerging ecowomanist thought provides a vital addition to ethical systems that too often leave communities of color on the margins of environmental dialogue. As an emergent academic field, it draws on womanist methodologies to diversify and radically strengthen the knowledge production that underlies our engagement with the complex, interconnected being that is our earth home. Ecowomanism leans into environmental justice, yet focuses on the ideas, values, and inherited environmental cultures that together shape how we function in relationship to, and as a part of, Earth. By centering ways of knowing in a diasporic community, ecowomanism seeks traditions and values that rehumanize women of color, center on our inherent agency, and celebrate our traditional roles as knowledge keepers in our communities to slow the impact of climate disruption. Ecowomanism seeks to build a new space of ethical engagement, one that prioritizes the lived experiences and inherited environmental cultures of women throughout the African diaspora in order to construct environmental ethics capable of changing our behaviors in response to environmental devastation. It does so in human-centered ways that remain vital to environmental justice, something I have long defined as *ethically anthropocentric*. As I explained in "Dishwater and the River: Toward an Ecowomanist Methodology,"

> I use the term *ethically anthropocentric* to make a distinction between anthropocentric religious ideas that imagine human beings as having an inherent dominion over all creation, privileging human comfort or extravagant lifestyles over the survival of entire ecosystems, and ethically anthropocentric approaches that prioritize certain human needs in order to remediate gross injustices within the human community that result from sacrificing certain marginalized groups. Such ethically prioritizable human needs come in response to what sociologists such as Robert Bullard define as environmental racism—the well-documented targeting of communities of color for the placement of toxic waste dumps, among other acts of environmental violence.[8] This corrupt and corrupting cycle

results in what womanist ethicist Emilie Townes refers to as the "contemporary . . . lynching [of] a whole people."[9] From an ethical perspective, environmental racism endangers not only the bodies of those in the target community but also the spirits of both those faced with horrendous choices and members of the broader community who live elsewhere and have numbed themselves against engagement with these issues. Organizing for the prevention of environmental destruction whose consequences are disproportionately inflicted upon certain marginalized communities is an example of an ethical, human-centered response to ecological devastation.[10]

Ecowomanist methodologies are therefore ethically anthropocentric approaches to repairing the natural world. By embracing theoethical approaches that draw on the inherent sacredness and vitality of creation while still prioritizing the work of dismantling racism, sexism, classism, and imperialism, womanist approaches to environmental ethics undermine environmental violence and hegemonic ideologies that posit peoples of African descent as having little care for environmental concerns.

Early womanist environmental scholarship focused almost entirely on wisdom drawn from the lived experiences of Black women in the United States. There remains fertile ground (and a great need) for growing ecowomanism to further embrace a transnational scope. Early geographic limitations in the field leave ecowomanism susceptible to racist ideologies that malign Black communities in the United States as less concerned about environmental issues than white communities. The insufficiently nuanced bias of such theories cries out for intersectional analysis.[11] The expansion of environmental ethics via a womanist lens not only must attend to the frequent exclusion of issues of race, gender, and class, but also must broaden womanist methodologies to engage environmental devastation through an understanding of diaspora. Not only are womanists accountable to impacted communities and silenced voices in the Global South, but we cede our engagement with the full array of ancestral wisdom at our peril. We too must learn new ways to tell stories in environmental time.

Postcolonial ecocritic Rob Nixon challenges us to understand how our ability to tell stories of environmental injustice and devastation, to resist apathy and sustain moral outrage over long periods of time, defines the very essence of our environmental engagement. Nixon defines the impact of environmental destruction on marginalized communities, particularly those facing poverty, as slow violence—"a violence that occurs gradually and out of sight, a violence of delayed destruction that is dispersed across time and space, an attritional violence that is typically not viewed as violence at all."[12] In *Slow Violence: The Environmentalism of the Poor*, Nixon considers slow violence as a critical framework for understanding the postcolonial deployment of environmentalism and globalization in the continued exploitation of the Global South by those in the Global North. This illuminating and badly needed paradigm, describing "formless threats whose fatal repercussions are dispersed across space and time,"[13] can be further utilized in exploring the interwoven robbing of agency and moral standing from West Indian migrant laborers and the environment itself that occurred during United States' construction of the Panamá Canal.

Nixon examines the work of writer-activists, engaging postcolonial literature as a strategy of representation that enables us to remain aware of the devastation, destruction, and injustice too often hidden from our perception by apathy and privileged cultural norms.[14] He does so in response to our "need to engage the representational, narrative, and strategic challenges posed by the relative invisibility of slow violence."[15] In essence, Nixon is challenging us to learn how to tell stories differently, to attend to politics of representation by utilizing a hermeneutic of suspicion in how we lend authority to particular voices in environmental debates. Nixon calls us to tell stories in "environmental time," in ways that are sustainably hearable over the long period of impact of such violent disruption.[16] And he insists that the cultural determinants of how we identify and empower those allowed to bear witness matter.[17]

Bearing witness, lifting the voices of those most impacted by oppression, and telling difficult stories over long periods of time are priorities that religious traditions are uniquely situated to address. Yet those same traditions must combat their own complacency and comfort with power and authority, embracing an ethic that privileges the wisdom of marginalized voices while investing in the agency and resacralization of those least valued in all of creation. When facing environmental devastation, religious institutions and scholars would benefit from womanist ethicist Emilie Townes's counterhegemonic approach in order to resituate religious tradition and moral teachings as tools that can participate in the healing of creation and promote the good. The development of religious environmental ethics has been addressed philosophically, theologically, and scripturally, but rarely in ways that engage the full impact of racial histories and formations on environmental devastation or on the likely effectiveness of our responses.

In *Womanist Ethics and the Cultural Production of Evil*, Townes skillfully weaves together a Foucauldian analysis of the fantastic with a Gramscian definition of hegemony to give name to the culture-constructing power of long-standing logics of domination. Her interventions expand on both to create working sites of intervention. By enlarging Foucault's imaginary from its creation via the written word to everyday experiences, Townes extracts its potency from the dormancy of literary documents to cultural constructions reencountered and reinscribed by our routine living. Those productive encounters can be used to dismantle self-sustaining narratives of domination and subordination. Townes emphasizes false moral universals as tools of power in her understanding of Gramsci's cultural hegemony, and further identifies countermemory as vital to the exclusion of false moral universals from ethical reflection.[18] The resulting "fantastic hegemonic imagination" she defines scribes the boundaries of societal evils normally too immense and amorphous to easily capture in words. She writes:

> The fantastic hegemonic imagination traffics in peoples' lives that are carica-tured or pillaged so that the imagination that creates the fantastic can control the world in its own image. This imagination conjures up worlds and their social structures that are not based on supernatural events and phantasms, but on the ordinariness of evil. It is this imagination, I argue, that helps to hold systematic, structural evil in place.[19]

Townes's work empowers ethical engagement with hegemonic structures sustained through potent cultural imaginaries. Ecowomanist ethics employs the fantastic hegemonic imagination by expanding the context of routine living to include the environment's connection to every aspect of existence.

Telling stories in environmental time requires us to consider the calamitous continuity of oppressive societal narratives over protracted intervals, stretch-ing ethical inquiry toward a planetary view. One might imagine that from the perspective of Earth's turning, historical periods characterized by chattel slavery, colonization, reconstruction, postcolonialism, civil rights, and cur-rent civil rights movements such as Black Lives Matter and the Movement for Black Lives are all arguably subject to the same counteroppressive analysis. Such assessment, I argue, identifies the most pernicious and tenacious log-ics of domination whose interminable repercussions continue to desecrate the environment and all others devalued through an imposed conflation with the natural world. This interminable sullying cries out for a wider perspec-tive. Collective racial memory is therefore fundamental to the recentering of wisdom from communities of the African diaspora in our response to envi-ronmental devastation. This work requires an exploration of environmental imaginaries broader than the wilderness tropes characterizing the majority of the American environmental canon. A dismantling of narratives colonizing tropical and jungle landscapes is vital to the work (see chapter 2).

Fortunately, dedicated scholars are broadening the scope of ecowomanist ethics. Melanie Harris, Delores Williams, Emilie Townes, Karen Baker-Fletcher, Layli Maparyan, Mercy Oduyoye, and Xiumei Pu, among others, are leading voices that have interrupted the unhelpful trope of Black communities as anti-environmentalist. Ecowomanist theoethicist Melanie Harris offers a comprehensive methodological approach for ecowomanist work in her foun-dational text *Ecowomanism: African American Women and Earth-Honoring*

Faiths that is grounded in the interreligious, diasporic work of liberation. Harris calls for a seven-step methodological approach: honoring experience and mining ecomemory, critically reflecting on experience and ecomemory, employing a womanist intersectional analysis, critically examining African and African American history and tradition, engaging transformation, sharing dialogue, and taking action for earth justice including the work of teaching ecowomanism.[20] Harris's methodology, while developed to engage African American women's Earth-honoring faiths, can be applied to transnational ecowomanist scholarship because of its comprehensive approach that is broad enough to allow for archival repair, the impact of migration on identity development, the use of family histories, the validation of multiple mythographies (see below), the reclamation of inherited environmental cultures, analyses that are not only intersectional but also decolonial, and the prioritization of the voices of Black women echoing through the historical record. It allows the work of ecowomanism to engage long-standing transnational histories of oppression.

The reality of environmental devastation catastrophically amplifies many conditions of marginalization. This shared devaluation is in no way inherent to nonhuman nature or other disempowered states of being. Instead, it is the legacy of what environmental philosopher Val Plumwood describes as a master narrative of Western culture. She describes this narrative as an anti-ecological rationalism that defends the primacy of reason through dualisms that equate subordinate constructions with the natural world.[21] Pairing reason with nature, mind with body, male with female, master with slave, civilized with primitive, rationality with animality, and so forth, Plumwood traces principal markers of oppression in Western culture. The exact form and context of the pairings shift over time yet bear "the layers of sediment deposited by past oppressions" in the intellectual history of dualistic thinking.[22]

Ultimately, dualisms evolve into ontological distinctions, where particular identities are defined as Other, as inherently separate from the hegemonic norm. The master narrative wields the power of history to define otherized groups as perpetually inferior and justify their unequal treatment in society.[23] This construction relies time and again on descriptions of oppressed groups as intrinsically animal-like, as closer to nature than to reason. According to Plumwood,

> Racism, colonialism and sexism have drawn their conceptual strength from casting sexual, racial, and ethnic difference as closer to the animal and the body construed as a sphere of inferiority, as a lesser form of humanity lacking the full measure of rationality or culture. . . . To be defined as "nature" in this context is to be defined as passive, as non-agent and non-subject, as the "environment" or invisible background conditions against which the "foreground" achievements

of reason or culture (provided typically by the white, western male expert or entrepreneur) take place. It is to be defined as a *terra nullius*, a resource empty of its own purposes or meanings, and hence available to be annexed for the purposes of those supposedly identified with reason or intellect, and to be conceived and moulded in relation to these purposes.[24]

Ecowomanist ethics is uniquely situated to interrupt the discourse of an anti-ecological master narrative. If we are to impact the course of environmental devastation, we must undermine the cultural productions of those ideologies most responsible for perpetuating structures of evil through domination.

METHODOLOGY

Constructing an ecowomanist ethic at the Panamá Canal further requires a diasporic multireligious epistemology with an analysis that reclaims inherited environmental cultural values; offers a transgenerational and transnational understanding of human identity drawn from creolized constructions of race, gender, class, and relationship to Earth; and repairs the archival record by engaging multiple mythographies (see below) in the construction of new knowledge. This work builds on Harris's solid methodological foundation, which rightly takes an interdisciplinary approach to center personal story, intersectional analyses, countermemory, and history and tradition from African peoples in transformative knowledge production.[25] Building on Harris's method requires an acknowledgment of the complexities in uncovering the lived experiences of migrant Caribbean women to Panamá during the initial US period of canal construction and the three decades following, when the impact of their arrival on succeeding generations' environmental values can be seen.

The erasure and vilification of these women's histories, lived realities, inherited environmental cultures, and struggles find hope of restoration and rehumanization in the methodology employed by Caribbean literary scholar Rhonda D. Frederick for the reconstruction of West Indian lives during the same time period. Frederick, one of the early scholars whose work rescues the untold stories of Caribbean migrant laborers on the Panamá Canal, centers narrative study and the engagement of cultural imaginaries to overcome the disciplinary limitations of colonial history.[26] Her interdisciplinary approach calls for the study of multiple mythographies, "literature, songs, histories, and memoirs about the twentieth-century migration of Caribbean people to the isthmus of Panamá," to reclaim the silenced stories that coexist with formal histories in the archival record.[27] This too is an expression of countermemory that strives to dismantle the impact of colonized ideologies that too often define the accepted boundaries of academic disciplines. Frederick describes multiple mythographies as

> a mythographic approach to the study of Caribbean isthmian workers, [that] therefore, offers insight into experiences that are not available in any one narrative form. Such an approach is particularly important for stories—and characters—that are not adequately represented in *any* isthmaian narrative.[28]

My construction of an ecowomanist ethic interweaves multiple narratives into a collective argument centered on the lived experiences of West Indian women at the site of the Panamá Canal. Its embrace of numerous voices from a variety of social locations to recover the echoes of late nineteenth- and early twentieth-century Caribbean experiences allows for archival repair that would otherwise prove impossible.

The use of multiple mythographies further disambiguates old tropes that rely on the conflation of Black women's bodies and Earth to the detriment of both. As women's studies scholar Katherine McKittrick proclaims in her revolutionary work on women's studies through the lens of geography,

> I am interested in thinking about the "close ties" between black women and geography because the connection reveals, as mentioned, how bodily geography can be. While the geographies of black women are certainly not always about flesh, or embodiment, the legacy of racism and sexism demonstrates how social systems organize seeable or public bodily differences.[29]

Kittredge draws on the work of M. NourbeSe Philip's writings on bodymemory and body silence to offer a methodological approach that assumes that "bodymemory is passed down and reinterpreted through generational remembrances, teachings, forewarnings, and advice. . . . Bodymemory is a corporeal continuity, which moves through time and recognizes where 'permanent' racial-sexual time-spaces appear in dominant texts."[30] Such an approach makes visible the silenced spaces in the historical archives, drawing on Black women's embodied epistemologies as *architectonic texts*, as Cannon would say. This analytic lens, paired with the multiple mythographies recommended by Fredericks's approach, opens literal landscapes of knowing as foundations for ecowomanist work.

Multilayered primary source materials require a holistic conceptual framework with the capacity to address the vibrant evolution of womanist epistemologies and methodologies. In her work to define ecowomanist theoethical approaches, Harris compellingly draws on the idea of *lifesystems* as providing us with agency and ingenuity in womanist ideas, "new language that fits us," to allow a broader context for a third-wave womanism. Her goal is the development of a third-wave womanism that reaches beyond the foundational Christian roots of early womanist thought to a religio-spiritual ecosystem that might just prove broad enough to reshape the human behaviors catalyzing the crisis of climate disruption.[31] Harris convincingly draws on Layli Maparyan's argument for a lifesystems approach to womanist thought writ large, via a neologism that reaches for meaning making more broadly than the constructs of formal religious traditions alone. Maparyan describes a lifesystem as "both a thought form and a thought community" and further explains:

> As such, it may contain institutions (such as religion), but is not constrained by them. More important is the thought architecture that ultimately produces those outward manifestations that come to be known as traditions, religions, or faiths. A lifesystem, then, encompasses both institutional and personal expressions of a particular understanding of humans, life, and creation in sacred or transcendental context. Such an understanding is cocreated and shared by a number of people throughout time and across space. The concept of lifesystems is useful here because it allows us to begin imagining how a global network of people who share nothing more than a common thought architecture about spirituality might collectively influence the shape of human society and life on Planet Earth merely by the power of their ideas.[32]

This important advance not only guides a broader analysis but also beautifully echoes Earth wisdom in its matrix of structures that mirror the very ecosystems we long to protect. Such an approach offers room enough for a reconstruction born of multiple mythographies without limiting reclaimed wisdom to that which fits within the very religious understandings that environmental ethicists like Willis Jenkins identify as coming into being in a time when we could not conceive of the human power to (re)shape geological history (see chapter 4).

While a lifesystems approach contextualizes a badly needed diversity in ecowomanist epistemologies, the ability to address interrelated, creolized religious and spiritual practices within those lifesystems remains. For such theoethical constructions, this project turns to the unifying worldview of organic multireligiosity. Ecowomanism provides life-giving arguments for championing an organic multireligiosity in its approach to reclaiming environmental values over time. Rather than requiring a religious ethic to conform to the creedal and doctrinal requirements of just one faith tradition while attempting to construct a system of values and responsibilities that are effective in guiding the environmental choices of diverse communities spanning a range of religious beliefs, organic multireligiosity (a term coined by Islamic and cultural studies scholar Ibrahim Abdurrahman Farajajé) "interrupts practices of considering religions as monolithic, rigidly-separated traditions in conflict with one another [and] rather understands them as having complex and constantly-morphing relationships in successive generations and in ever-widening geographical and cultural contexts."[33] This disruption of absolutist approaches to morality, which simultaneously widens our acknowledgment of religious valuation, allows for constructive reimaginings of interrelated faith traditions to amplify our ability to re-story our histories of environmental self-knowing.

Such a re-storying, deeply grounded in practices of countermemory, becomes critical in the struggle to remain faithful to our environmental commitments, whatever they may be. Townes argues for a strategy of countermemory in dismantling hegemonic domination along class, gender, and racial lines. For Townes,

> countermemory seeks to open up not only the subversive spaces of counterhegemony, it argues also for a reconstitution of history such that we begin to see, hear, and appreciate the diversities in our midst as flesh and blood rather than as cloying distractions.[34]

Her work forges new ethical ground by which to analyze and undermine the hegemonic norms clouding our understandings of the good and the right in our societal relations, public policy decisions, and the commodification of identity. She does so in part by insisting on the particularity of perspective that is central to a womanist ethical approach.[35] Townes's attention to the power of a national imaginary in constructing and maintaining hegemonic dominance is uniquely suited to a study that requires the recovery and repair of knowledge hidden by a century of moralistic dissembling.

Melanie Harris clearly defines ecomemory, the recovery of what I would term inherited environmental cultures in relation to Earth itself, as a type of countermemory.[36] Emphasizing countermemory within an ecowomanist methodology in order to interrogate tropical triumphalism through the lived experiences of Black women laboring in connection with the Panamá Canal's construction provides a critical contradistinction for the creation of a transnational womanist environmental ethic. This study draws on Harris's ecowomanist method and expands her call for ecomemory, the reconstitution of environmental history to include the voices and lived experiences of African peoples,[37] by adding the reclamation of inherited environmental cultures. It further elevates not only African peoples and African American peoples but also the creolized island communities of the Caribbean as key sites of understanding identity and environmental justice across the African diaspora. The work of slowing climate disruption requires a change in daily life practices. It requires not only the too often silenced environmental stories of our communities but also the recovery of traditions and practices that call us into our own knowing. Inherited environmental cultures, which can be understood as a specific subset of ecomemory that transcends history, center the very customs that sustain behavioral change.

This work promotes engagement with what I am calling ecocreolization, a shifting and blending of identity as separate communities build a new shared understanding of self in the face of violent acts of forced displacement and multigenerational legacies of harm. This emergence of new cultural understandings necessarily includes our communal relationship with Earth. It is the work of countermemory that is central to sustaining behavioral change in the face of climate devastation, and an uncompromising act of decolonization. Ecocreolization acts as an agential force that builds knowledge through shared experience and survival on new lands. Such agency in the face of oppression wielded along the lines of race, gender, class, and our relationship to Earth cries out for a reexamination of what we know of our own humanity. This project therefore centers on the development of an ecowomanist moral anthropology to sustain human responses to climate disruption in environmental time.

As a result, *Ecowomanism at the Panamá Canal* is indebted to the field of postcolonial ecocriticism. Postcolonial ecocriticism and womanist theoethics intersect at the use of literature (and art writ large) to study the transmission of cultural knowledge. While both utilize cultural expression as a generative source, ecowomanism insists that engagement with postcolonial literature alone is insufficient. We are further called to reread history itself through an anti-imperial lens and with a commitment to archival repair. The use of multiple mythographies as a methodological approach becomes vital in contexts where inherited cultural wisdom is sought from voices of the routinely silenced. Communication through such dehumanization and across generations is a revolutionary act. The least we can do as inheritors of such agential courage is insist on a storied history read through a decolonial lens. Our great writers offer us a glimpse into futures beyond the imagining of our current moment. Our ancestors offer us blueprints for surviving the unimaginable, and through our very existence bear witness to the birthing of new ways. Ecowomanism insists that we are more than capable of the sustained cultural shift and behavioral practices that might redistribute the consequences of environmental destruction in equitable ways. It does so by centering the hard-won words of those who bore the unspeakable. The promise of such possibility is found in our very existence on the planet.

Harris's method further expands the womanist expectation that scholars situate their research in relation to our own identities and lived experiences by modeling the inclusion of ecoautobiographies and family ecojourneys in our work. We are the ones who can assist with recounting the ecoautobiographies of our foremothers that were too often silenced and rewritten by racist capitalist patriarchs whose rapacious settler colonialist worldviews drove the competition to exploit Earth's resources. It is ours to gather seeds left behind in conditions unfavorable for growth and sow them in gardens of possibility our mothers could only dream about at times. In our planting, we must remember the power of their ability to "make do." My evolving ecoautobiography is below. I am blessed to have women in my extended family, born in the days of Panamá Canal construction, offer a piece of our family's ecojourney in their own words (see chapter 3).

ECOAUTOBIOGRAPHY

I am a first-generation daughter of Chilean and Panamanian immigrants to the United States. My story is inherently one of environmental displacement, with tensions stretching between the outrageous overconsumption of the Global North and the profound need for decolonization as healing and recovery in the lived environmental histories of the Global South. I was raised in Manhattan, and was blessed with frequent opportunities to spend summers in Pennsylvania, go on camping trips to many national parks in the eastern United States, and visit family in both Chile and Panamá. My international connections to family expanded my sense of Earth from the urban rhythms of New York City to the volcanic lakes of Chile and the rainforests of Panamá. My identity as a middle-class, queer, multiracial, and multiethnic (Latina and African descent) cisgender woman living in the Global North has a significant impact on my collusion with climate disruption and the privilege through which I engage environmental devastation. I am an ordained Unitarian Universalist minister, and my tradition encourages me to embrace pluralistic theological responses to global crises. My own research is situated in the emergent field of ecowomanism, specifically in ecowomanist ethics, in that I seek to develop environmental ethics drawn from the lived experiences of women of color, particularly those from the African diaspora. It draws on feminist intercultural theologies from womanist, mujerista, and Latina feminist thinkers both within and outside the academy. My conception of Blackness is broad, tracing the African diasporic stories of survival and thriving across the globe.

I credit my father for my strong sense of self in relation to Earth even though I spent my youth in primarily urban environments. He took me into natural spaces at every opportunity and nurtured my fascination with life in all its forms. I remember the importance as a child living in New York City of watching the moon cycle through its waxing, fullness, waning, and absence in the night sky. The moon was the only natural light source in a city that was literally ablaze after nightfall. I remember collecting the hard seedpods of the honey locust trees each fall as the school year began. Those long, brown, flat seedpods that sound like maracas when you shake them reminded me somehow of my maternal grandmother, who always let me feed the seeds from whatever peppers she was cooking to the canary who took up residence in her home. I would carefully store the honey locust pods on a shelf in my bedroom so that they would dry out completely. Once dry, I would split them and plant the seeds carefully around the edges of my mother's potted plants. This was my garden on the twenty-first floor of an apartment building in Greenwich Village. I have memories of this back-to-school ritual from as long as I can remember going to school, which began before my third birthday. My poor mother kept vigil every year, but inevitably found baby trees growing all over the house. My childhood contained mighty forests in tiny pots.

It was important to me to plant something that was a part of my natural environment. As I planted seeds, I made connections. There were many other annual rituals, which were reminders of the larger web of life around me. For many years I spent a week in Pennsylvania with a close friend and we would pick four cups of blueberries (enough to make a pie) right at the end of each summer. I remember collecting clusters of red hawthorn berries to decorate our dining room table, also right at the start of the school year. Going to the botanical gardens to see the cherry blossoms with my father meant that the school year had almost finished, and I was reminded of that every time I entered Central Park and saw the same blossoms lining the path around the reservoir. The springtime ritual of spreading as many dandelion seeds (and with them wishes and prayers) as I could is one that I continue to this day.

These acts lent tangible reminders of my connection to Earth. They served the purpose of taking me out of my distracted everyday world, and allowed me to *touch* the Earth again, even in the middle of a city, as a sign of my communion, a visceral reminder. We have a longing—a deep inner yearning for connection to one another, to the life that surrounds us, and to our broader community and world. As our Earth-honoring faiths are called to respond to the realities of climate disruption, we find ourselves impacted by faithful longings, some of which drive us to reimagine our traditions in ways that promote climate justice. We are also impacted by the particular lived experiences and histories of the religious and secular communities actively engaging these issues. Liberation theologies build on those lived experiences and histories to call us to a reclamation of inherited environmental cultures and practices as a corrective to master narratives of dominance and globalization, thereby allowing the construction of multivocal, multireligious, multicultural global ethics in response to the problem of climate destruction.

The cultural inheritances that interest me most are found in everyday family stories, in old work songs and folk tales, in local interpretations of religious festivals and sacred scriptures. I believe that the same strength and grace that allowed many peoples to survive centuries of violence and the daily lived experience of bigotry and abuse in a white supremacist world also allowed for the transmission of pluralistic understandings of the sacred relationship between human and nonhuman nature. We reclaim such strength through the identification and recollection of the wisdom of all of our grandmothers.

My students often ask me how something as small as my Panamanian grandmother's practice of saving pepper seeds to feed the canary that flew into her porch one morning and made itself at home in her house can impact something as inconceivably large as climate disruption. Why might inherited environmental cultures matter profoundly to the earth justice-seeking behavioral changes that theological exploration has so far struggled to catalyze in our communities of faith? My understanding of culture is broader than one practice, habit, or act. My grandmother's seed-saving response—choosing to reserve something out of her own regular sources of food that she might otherwise have planted or simply thrown away rather than chasing a bird "out of place," as it were, back out the door of her home—speaks volumes to me about neighbor love, survival, and particularly West Indian value of "making do." All of these fed into lessons I learned as a four year old being handed the top of a pepper I could not identify and told to be careful with the seeds as I took them to the hungry canary. I believe we must rediscover, gather together, rename, and repurpose our *own* resources for once—the environmental living and learning that is long silenced by dominant cultures and traditions of destruction and misuse. If all of us bring such wisdom to the table, share it with strangers, and open ourselves up to creative moral possibilities, we might find a common cooperative ground on which to faithfully respond to environmental devastation.

Lastly, my ancestors' hands helped to dig the "big ditch," as Panamanians often refer to the Panamá Canal. Their pride in overcoming the impossible remains of utmost importance to me. While this project critiques the environmental impact and ideologies of manifest destiny and tropical triumphalism that drove the development of the American empire at the site of the canal, it in no way intends to minimize the perseverance, strength, or profound resilience of those migrants whose physical labors accomplished the unimaginable. At the Miraflores Locks in Panamá, there is a searchable database of laborers whose names appear in the official historic record. Sadly, I cannot find any women in my family on these lists as their labors and names were rarely recognized by the US government. Yet a search for my mother's surname, just one branch of my family that migrated from Jamaica and Barbados to work on the canal, returns Edward and Joseph Lynton to my immediate memory, who migrated to Panamá in 1906 and 1909, respectively.

It also matters that until my mother received her US citizenship in 2002, I was the only US citizen on either side of my nuclear family and certainly within a few close generations of my Panamanian family. I grew up with a naïve understanding of Panamá on many levels, but particularly on the environmental level. My first engagement with environmental issues in Panamá mainly came through the lens of ecotourism. I heard the stories of foolhardy Americans who romanticized the rainforest and their own power within it and regularly got lost while hiking. The stories of bugs taking their revenge were told with some real glee. My family is still working on the canal today, but instead of laboring in its construction, they serve primarily as pilots and engineers.

"LITTLE TRINKLES OF WATER": WHY THE PANAMÁ CANAL

As a site of inquiry, the Panamá Canal adds to the framework of womanist ethics and allows for the inclusion of my own family histories and social locations to contribute a Caribbean diasporic perspective to (eco)womanist scholarship. It represents a concrete site of environmental devastation, extreme human intervention in the form of uniting two oceans for the first time in geological history, a richly complex, multilayered example of ecocreolization, and a historical site of US neo-imperialism. Of added importance to current issues in environmental ethics as a whole, the Panamá Canal exemplifies many of the devastating decisions that remain when a resource has been historically situated in the Global South but controlled by a foreign ruling power in the Global North. The canal's return to the Panamanian government in 1999 raises vital questions that would benefit from a locally informed environmental ethics.[38] How do we address the often competing issues of human rights, the rights of nonhuman nature, environmental repair, economic development, and the ongoing quest for "progress"? What wisdom remains to be drawn from the environmental cultures carried by a forcibly displaced community into diaspora? And who is responsible for the damage that has already occurred?

The Panamá Canal is also considered one of the seven wonders of the modern world. Its inclusion on this list of engineering achievements compiled by the American Society of Civil Engineers in 1994 speaks to the power of the imaginaries surrounding its construction. Its narratives differ greatly when told from the perspective of American ingenuity, versus that of West Indian resilience, versus that of its impact on Earth. Canal narratives from an Earth perspective are rare, and unlikely to include moral agency. Yet monuments as a whole are frequently imbued with the weight of morality, existing as symbols of our highest ideals.[39] Such narratives blur the lines between the common good and the sanitation of evil in the form of domination.

There can be no question that the Panamá Canal has a massive environmental impact. Whether boats cross from the Pacific Ocean in the south or the Atlantic in the north, they traverse a series of three locks while crossing the isthmus. US engineers built a massive dam in 1911 to block the natural flow of the Chagres River to the Atlantic Ocean. The resulting floodwaters created Gatún Lake as the largest water reservoir to power the lock system of the canal, displacing both human and nonhuman nature. Gatún Lake stretches over 164 square miles and still does not store sufficient water to sustain modern traffic through the canal. It takes 52 million gallons of freshwater to move just one boat through the Panamá Canal in its current configuration. The water is funneled from rainfall across the 1,077-square-mile watershed surrounding the canal and stored in Gatún Lake and—as of the 1930s, in preparation for the first canal expansion—Lake Alajuela. An average of thirty-five to forty-five ships pass through the canal on any given day.[40] All of that displaced water, and any aquatic life that it contains, gets dumped into the salt waters of the oceans on either side of the canal. I have witnessed gulls fishing in the canal as ships wait patiently for the locks to raise or lower them to cross through to the next section. The canal has operated 365 days a year with almost no exceptions for over a century now. In a country where an average of 130 inches of rain falls annually, water shortages now occur at times during the dry season from both increased canal traffic and population growth. In 1997, canal authorities had to limit the cargo capacity of ships for the first time in the canal's history due to lack of water.[41]

The creation of Gatún Lake diverted rivers, changed microclimates, and displaced populations. As traditional farming communities in the western part of the country lost their livelihoods due to the desiccation of the land in the tropics (the last place a water shortfall should occur), there was significant movement into new urban areas. Environmental anthropologist Ashley Carse powerfully illustrates the immense water consumption of the canal by narrating the water cost of just one ship crossing between oceans:

> While passing through the locks, each ship that transits the canal drains an astonishing *52 million gallons of fresh water* into the oceans—approximately the same volume of water as in 78 Olympic swimming pools, 15 million toilet flushes, or the daily domestic consumption of half of a million Panamanians.[42]

As is all too common in economic ventures with significant environmental impacts, the diminishment of freshwater in the area has never been incorporated into cost analyses for the utilization of the canal. The United States did not pay any fees for its 94 percent share of water usage drawn from the Panamá Canal basin to operate the canal. The 1977 Torrijos–Carter Treaties, which mapped out a twenty-two-year transition agreement for control of the Panamá Canal to revert to Panamá from the United States at the close of 1999, guaranteed the negation of this natural resource cost by requiring that Panamá provide all the water needed to operate the canal at no cost to the United States. The small fees collected from ships traversing the canal and water usage fees of Panamanian residents have zero allocation for the protection of the watershed.[43]

This environmental story is also primarily one where the tensions between a human-centered valuation and utilization of the isthmus and the way Earth arguably strives to remain in balance can be observed in the recollections of those who witnessed the massive geological changes that came with canal construction. The mindset of witnesses who believed canal construction worked to restore Earth to a type of proper purpose underscores the tropical triumphalism of an American story of engineering prowess in building the canal itself. British geographer Vaughan Cornish, whose extensive writings emphasize the supposed importance and utility of imperial efforts, wrote primarily of the challenges of Panamá Canal construction as the need to control the uncooperative aspects of Earth itself. His perspective was common among those whose labors were seen as a mighty battle against a recalcitrant landscape. Cornish describes the need to control the rivers in Panamá both by disposing of excess water in the rainy season and utilizing stored rainfall to remediate evaporation and water wasted by the locks in the dry season. For Cornish, the work of excavation was a tireless effort at restructuring Earth itself, and his disparagement of the soil that plagued the canal's completion clearly depicts a common devaluation of the land. He writes of the dirt as that "which stands between the American nation and the realization of their long-cherished scheme, and nowhere is the classical definition of dirt as 'matter in the wrong place' so appropriate as on the Isthmus."[44]

Elizabeth Kittredge Parker, whose husband worked as a canal official during the initial US period of construction, describes the immediate impact of waters from the manufacture of Gatún Lake. Gatún Lake flooded with rainwater before the release of its waters in advance of the canal's formal opening on August 15, 1914. Parker's memoir, *Panama Canal Bride*, captures the details of the water's redirection.

Then came the historic day when the water was to be turned into the Canal channel. The dyke at Gamboa, built across the channel where the Chagres River entered the Canal, had kept the rising water of the lake from the Cut. Now, its job was finished, like that of the steam shovels and little line towns. It must be destroyed. It was a bright sunny day on October, 1913. On special trains, all who could rushed to the banks of the river near the dyke. We held our breath as the clocks ticked the minutes away. At the appointed time,

President Wilson in Washington touched the key, giving the signal. Then, like a sleeping giant, rudely awakened, the dyke became alive, the dirt was blown to the sky, and the unfettered waters surged into the Canal channel—into Culebra Cut.

Gradually, little trinkles of water from the Atlantic met little trinkles of water from the Pacific, merging and rising until the water in the Cut was of sufficient depth for dredges, which took over from the shovels the work of excavation.

As the lake rose higher and higher, a constant patrol was necessary to drive the natives back to the hills. And back to the hills fled all tropic life. The monkeys, the tapirs, the snakes, the weird insects, even the lazy sloths, all fled to the hills, which were made islands by the oncoming waters. Only the mighty hardwood trees remained, their bare branches stretching over the blue water— ghostly reminders of a once-teeming jungle.[45]

The *Canal Record*, a weekly paper run by the Isthmian Canal Commission, confirms that at 2:02 p.m. on October 10, 1913, a signal rigged from a lever depressed by US president Woodrow Wilson in Washington, DC, and transmitted by telegraph, submarine cable, and a transisthmian cable to a local circuit tripped a switch to set off the dynamite.[46]

Both the need for the president's own hand to blast a 125-foot gap in the dike and the common imagery of a war against Earth speak to the rise of tropical triumphalism in Panamá, which I explore further in chapter 2. Caribbean scholar Olive Senior preserves US engineer Edward Young's memory of that day, who bears witness to both the wounding of the land and the elation of those gathered in celebration.

I remember the bottom of the Cut that morning, three hundred feet wide and flat with a deep drainage-ditch in the exact centre . . . a yawning gash nine miles long and over six hundred feet deep at Gold Hill, a great scar into the very vitals of Nature. . . . *Boom! Boom! Boom-boom! Boom-boom-boom!* came the muffled reports of the dynamite bombs that had been placed along the face of Gamboa dike. The water shot upward in a foaming cataract, visible for miles. Then came the coffee-colored flood raging through the Cut.

Cheer on cheer. Men were screaming mad with joy. The shouts welded together in a mighty roar that echoed above the roar of water tearing through the Cut.[47]

The language and narratives of connecting two oceans through human intervention for the first time in geological history speak solely to engineering prowess and US control with little acknowledgment of environmental impact beyond an odd sort of crowd control. Yet a 1919 image of the corpses of trees

Figure 1.1 *The Dying Jungle—Gatún Lake, February 1919,* **from the collection of Lesley Hendricks.** "Picture of the Week," CZ Brats, March 12, 2001, https://www.czbrats .com/PicWk/PkWk76.htm. *Source:* Lesley Hendricks.

still standing in Gatún Lake is a heart-rending reminder of the true consequences of such hubris (see figure 1.1).

LIMITATIONS OF THE PROJECT

This project constructs a transnational ecowomanist ethic that reclaims inherited environmental cultures across multiple sites of displacement at the site of the Panamá Canal. It is not intended to offer a comprehensive history of canal construction or West Indian migration to Panamá, nor an in-depth environmental impact study. There already exist excellent examples of all three, with recent additions of powerful scholarship that reclaim the silenced histories of West Indian laborers who migrated to Panamá to work on the canal. This study is indebted to the work of many scholars, named within its pages, whose efforts allow for gleaning narratives through an environmental lens to support the development of an ecowomanist ethic. It further owes a debt of gratitude to the Smithsonian Tropical Research Institute for over a century of "increasing and sharing knowledge about the past, present and future of tropical ecosystems and their relevance to human welfare."[48] Established in Panamá in 1910, the Research Institute serves as a hub for science, education, and learning around the globe.

This study levels significant critique focused on imperial anti-Earth ideologies, particularly those espoused by the US government and its citizens during the time of canal construction. It both questions and mourns the profound environmental cost of building and operating the canal. In no way does it intend to question or criticize the immense labor of the West Indian community. Our community is rightly proud of all that it accomplished during the years of digging the "big ditch." The ideologies that drove the need for such labor were not ours. Our people expressed the values of legitimate work, support for family, education of our children, and pride in our resiliency and resolve. May we be ever gratified by those accomplishments.

Chapter 4 of this project draws on narratives of Obeah to construct an eco-womanist ethic. This study does not depict or list exhaustive examples of the specific practices of Obeah. Such anthropological cataloging is both outside the scope of this work and also intentionally omitted in order to honor the intellectual property and agency of Obeah practitioners. I am not an expert in such practices outside of those I have inherited from my own family and ancestral lines.

This project is limited by its historical context to engage with the narratives of cisgender women. I believe fervently, along with others in both fields, in the need to broaden both Latina feminist intercultural theologies and womanist theoethics to embrace a broader understanding of gender as a whole. I further assume that gender nonconforming people live in every age. Sadly, the hegemony of the gender binary serves to eliminate histories that would make us all more whole. This study is likely marred by traces of cissexism. I pledge to work to eradicate such injustice in my teaching and scholarship.

Lastly, this labor is also tainted by histories defiling the full humanity of sex workers. The narratives surrounding the so-called prostitution at the site of the Panamá Canal are themselves often violent and violating. While at times I use the language of sex work in this text, more often my writing defaults to the language of prostitution employed during the era being studied. I want to acknowledge the full humanity of sex workers and the truth of their labor. Sex work is work.

SELECTION OF TERMS

I have made many choices about the specific use of language over the course of this project. Often I default to a type of interculturality by weaving together multiple words for a range of identities, geographic areas, and life circumstances. The realities of chattel slavery and settler colonialism mean that much of our language is itself colonized. This section is an attempt to clarify a bit of my thinking, even where there exists no rehumanizing option in our shared languages.

West Indian: I use *West Indian* to refer to Black people from the anglophone Caribbean who migrated to Panamá. This is a very small and specific group of people, and I made this decision to honor my family and community that still refer to themselves in this way. I know nothing more powerful in the granting of agency than the right to name oneself. It is also the language that was used at the time. I agree with others that there is an inherent colonialism in this language. But it is not mine to change the words in the mouths of my family. I choose not to use *colored* to refer to our people, even though it was used in interviews by women in my extended family. This is because they corrected themselves in those interviews, explaining that the old language is sometimes hard to overcome.

Caribbean: I use *Caribbean* to describe the lands surrounding the Caribbean Sea. I only use this term geographically. When speaking of peoples of African descent who live or lived in the Caribbean, I refer to them as Black.

Black: There is no question that *Black* is often used as a pejorative term, one externally imposed on those with greater melanin in their skin. It is also a term that has been reclaimed with great pride. It serves as a diasporic designation that transcends the common default to *African American* when describing people from the African diaspora here in the Global North. *Black* is capitalized throughout the project as a visual reminder of agency and reclamation. As I say in the text, my conception of Blackness is broad. It is also rich, powerful, and fertile, like Earth itself.

Silver sisters: Velma Newton's important text, *The Silver Men: West Indian Labour Migration to Panama 1850–1914*, reclaims the identifier of "silver men" to honor the West Indians laboring on the canal.[49] These laborers faced injustice in the now well-documented discrepancy in pay between white workers, who were paid in gold, and Black laborers, who were paid in silver. I have witnessed West Indian women refer to our ancestors as silver women, or silver sisters. This powerful language serves to reestablish the contributions and labor of women at the canal. I use it in a chapter title to honor that powerful sense of worth.

American: My own family reminds me that America is not limited to the United States. I frequently use *American* in this project to refer to residents of the United States, or to their logics of identity, morality, and existence. I do this because the historical record is rife with this term being used to mean solely the continental United States. This use is pervasive in the history covered by this project. I do fully recognize with pride that the Americas are much larger than my own neo-imperial nation.

Creation: I often use the term *creation* to refer to all of existence in a way that carries a sacred valence. The capitalized *Creation* is often used to refer to specific Jewish and Christian teachings about the universe as coming into being through the will (or as an act) of God. I choose to reclaim the word *creation*, in all its organic multireligiosity, as a signpost to the inherent sacrality of all that is. It is an inherently universalist term, one that invites us to a more holistic understanding of our relationship with Earth.

Climate disruption, environmental devastation, and so forth: I use many terms to refer to the profound impact of human destruction on Earth. I believe they all have utility and cannot be used often enough to shake humanity from apathetic complacency.

Spanish language terms: I have chosen to eschew the common convention of italicizing non-English words. This is to disrupt and decolonize academic norms about the languages and words readers are expected to understand.

CHAPTER SUMMARIES

Chapter 1 lays out the specifics of developing an ecowomanist ethic at the site of the Panamá Canal. It builds on the ecowomanist methodology of Melanie Harris and argues that transnational ecowomanism should be intercultural, decolonial, organically multireligious, and equipped to encompass multiple mythographies. This chapter contains my own ecoautobiography, as well as a brief environmental impact history of the canal that models a narrative approach.

Chapter 2 draws on countermemory to offer an ecowomanist response to tropical triumphalism. It argues for the inclusion of imperialism as part of a fourfold counteroppressive foundation for womanist study. This chapter interrogates ideologies used to conscript Black women's bodies and Earth itself. It places those ideologies in the specific geographic landscape of Panamá and engages the lived histories of women from Martinique whose arrival to Panamá in 1905 is emblematic of the ways women are vilified through moralistic tropes concerning sex work.

Chapter 3 engages multiple mythographies of the lived experiences of West Indian women during the construction of the Panamá Canal to offer *ecocreolization* as an intervention in the work of environmental ethics. This chapter engages the 1926 anthology of cartoonish depictions of the canal zone *Macwalbax: A Collection of Poems, Cartoons, and Comment*; Elizabeth Kittredge Parker's 1955 memoir *Panama Canal Bride*; and video-recorded interviews of women in my extended family to probe narratives of West Indian women's experiences and inherited environmental cultures.

Chapter 4 develops an ecowomanist moral anthropology that engages questions of dignity, relationality, and environmental justice. This ecowomanist moral anthropology serves as a theoethical understanding of human nature and its intrinsic interrelatedness with all of creation. This chapter addresses womanist Earth-honoring epistemologies by proposing the reclamation of the diasporic practices collectively labeled as *Obeah* for the identification of cultural inheritances and knowledge production that offer agency, accountability, and a material grounding in the natural world. This chapter resolves in the construction of an ecowomanist ethic at the site of the Panamá Canal.

NOTES

1. "Canal Heroes," Miraflores Visitor Center, Panamá City, Panamá. Informational display.
2. Ada María Isasi-Díaz, *Mujerista Theology: A Theology for the Twenty-First Century* (New York: Orbis Books, 1996), 64–66.
3. María Cristina Ventura Campusano, "Between Oppression and Resistance: From the Capture of the Imaginary to the Journey of the Intercultural," in *Feminist Intercultural Theology: Latina Explorations for a Just World,* ed. María Pilar Aquino and Maria José Rosado-Nunes (New York: Orbis Books, 2007), 179.
4. Nancy Elizabeth Bedford, "Making Spaces: Latin American and Latina Feminist Theologies on the Cusp of Interculturality," in *Feminist Intercultural Theology,* ed. Aquino and Rosado-Nunes, 58–59.
5. Olga Consuelo Vélez Caro, "Toward a Feminist Intercultural Theology," in *Feminist Intercultural Theology,* ed. Aquino and Rosado-Nunes, 256–57.
6. For Katie Cannon's development of Black women's literature as a source for womanist ethics, see Katie Cannon, *Katie's Canon: Womanism and the Soul of the Black Community* (New York: Continuum International, 2008), 63–65.
7. Jeanette Rodríguez, "Tripuenteando: Journey toward Identity, the Academy, and Solidarity," in *Feminist Intercultural Theology,* ed. Aquino and Rosado-Nunes, 75.
8. Robert Bullard, "Environmental Justice in the Twenty-First Century," in *The Quest for Environmental Justice: Human Rights and the Politics of Pollution,* ed. Robert Bullard (San Francisco: Sierra Club Books, 2005), 32–34.
9. Emilie Townes, *In a Blaze of Glory: Womanist Spirituality as Social Witness* (Nashville: Abingdon Press, 1995), 55.
10. Sofía Betancourt, "Between Dishwater and the River: Toward an Ecowomanist Methodology," in *Ecowomanism, Religion, and Ecology,* ed. Melanie Harris (Leiden: Brill, 2017), 62.
11. William Arp III and Keith Boeckelman, "Religiosity: A Source of Black Environmentalism and Empowerment?," *Journal of Black Studies* 28, no. 2 (November 1997): 257.
12. Rob Nixon, *Slow Violence and the Environmentalism of the Poor* (Boston: Harvard University Press, 2011), 2.
13. Nixon, *Slow Violence,* 10.

14. Nixon, *Slow Violence*, 14–15.

15. Nixon, *Slow Violence*, 2.

16. Nixon, *Slow Violence*, 47.

17. Nixon, *Slow Violence*, 16.

18. Emilie Townes, *Womanist Ethics and the Cultural Production of Evil* (New York: Palgrave Macmillan, 2006), 18–21, 52.

19. Townes, *Womanist Ethics*, 21.

20. Melanie L. Harris, *Ecowomanism: African American Women and Earth-Honoring Faiths* (New York: Orbis Books, 2017), 27–59.

21. Val Plumwood, *Environmental Culture: The Ecological Crisis of Reason* (New York: Routledge, 2002), 18–19.

22. Val Plumwood, *Feminism and the Mastery of Nature* (New York: Routledge, 1993), 42–43.

23. Plumwood, *Environmental Culture,* 102–03.

24. Plumwood, *Feminism and the Mastery*, 4.

25. For further explanation of ecowomanist methodology, see Harris, *Ecowomanism*, chapter 2.

26. Rhonda D. Frederick, *"Colón Man a Come": Mythographies of Panamá Canal Migration* (Lanham, MD: Lexington Books, 2005), ix–xi.

27. Frederick, *"Colón Man a Come,"* 3.

28. Frederick, *"Colón Man a Come,"* 198.

29. Katherine McKittrick, *Demonic Grounds: Black Women and the Cartographies of Struggle* (Minneapolis: University of Minnesota Press, 2006), 45–46.

30. McKittrick, *Demonic Grounds*, 49.

31. Harris, *Ecowomanism*, 112.

32. Layli Maparyan, *The Womanist Idea* (New York: Routledge, 2012), 92.

33. Ibrahim Farajajé, "Organic Multireligiosity and Seriously (Warning: Coloured) Organic Scholarship," Facebook, August 26, 2012, https://www.facebook.com/notes/khalvat-dar-anjuman/organic-multireligiosity-and-seriously-warning-coloured-organic-scholarship/10151226711691579/.

34. Townes, *Womanist Ethics*, 21.

35. Townes, *Womanist Ethics,* 23.

36. Harris, *Ecowomanism*, 28, 31–32.

37. Harris, *Ecowomanism*, 31–32.

38. Richard W. Van Alstyne, "The Panama Canal: A Classical Case of Imperial Hangover," *Journal of Contemporary History* 15, no. 2 (April 1980): 300–01, https://doi.org/10.1177/002200948001500205.

39. David M. Smith, *Moral Geographies: Ethics in a World of Difference* (Edinburgh: Edinburgh University Press, 2000), 46.

40. Ashley Carse, "Nature as Infrastructure: Making and Managing the Panama Canal Watershed," *Social Studies of Science* 42, no. 4 (2012): 539–40, 547–48, https://doi.org/10.1177/0306312712440166.

41. Mark Brooks, "Economic Growth, Ecological Limits, and the Proposed Expansion of the Panama Canal" (master's thesis, McGill University, 2005), 12–13.

42. Ashley Carse, *Beyond the Big Ditch: Politics, Ecology, and Infrastructure at the Panama Canal* (Cambridge, MA: MIT Press, 2014), 3.

43. Stanley Heckadon Moreno, "Impact of Development on the Panama Canal Environment," in "The Future of Panama and the Canal," ed. Richard L. Millett, special issue, *Journal of Interamerican Studies and World Affairs* 35, no. 3 (Autumn 1993): 145–46, https://doi.org/10.2307/165971.

44. Vaughan Cornish, "The Panama Canal in 1908," *Geographical Journal* 33, no. 2 (February 1909): 162, 167.

45. Elizabeth Kittredge Parker, *Panama Canal Bride: A Story of Construction Days* (New York: Exposition Press, 1955), 81–82.

46. "Destruction of Last Dike," *Canal Record*, October 15, 1913, 65–66.

47. Olive Senior, *Dying to Better Themselves: West Indians and the Building of the Panama Canal* (Kingston: University of the West Indies Press, 2014), 3.

48. "About Us," Smithsonian Tropical Research Institute, accessed January 18, 2020, https://stri.si.edu/about-us.

49. Velma Newton, *The Silver Men: West Indian Labour Migration to Panama 1850–1914* (Kingston: Ian Randle, 2004), 122.

Chapter 2

Geography, Countermemory, and Resistance

Over the course of the twentieth century, the efforts of the United States to successfully construct a canal across the Isthmus of Panamá gained the hegemonic weight of legend as a story defining US progress, dominion, and engineering might. Its uninterrogated rootedness in American ideologies of manifest destiny and tropical triumphalism masks a Protestant ethic of control that continues to influence environmental decision-making a century later, even after jurisdiction over the canal returned to the Panamanian government.[1] This legend plays a definitive role in the justification of US expansionism at the start of the twentieth century. Historian Julie Green argues convincingly in her laudable work *The Canal Builders: Making America's Empire at the Panama Canal* that the successful construction of the Panamá Canal replaced morally questionable images of the American empire with a positive national identity centered on benevolence, progress, and strength. As Green writes, "The canal project became a signal moment in the building of America's new empire, and it also became a moment wrapped up inextricably with idealism and notions of selfless gifts to civilization."[2] Her work identifies the canal as a tool central to the successful development of a new American empire that at the same time legitimized a national narrative that masks US imperialism to this day.[3] Moral certitude became the dividing line between the positive vision of a growing global power and neatly sidestepped accusations of neo-imperialism.

Critical to this analysis are the additional factors of the canal's ongoing environmental impact (as discussed in chapter 1), along with the environmental tropes used to secure such moral and cultural high ground. Progress at the canal became the subject of national fascination in the United States, and the benevolent overtones of a growing tropical imaginary relied on interconnected assumptions of the racial and environmental superiority of US whites.

Consequently, the stories of the land and those who labored upon it cannot be dissociated from such a lasting story of American triumph. While recent scholarship has made outstanding advances in the histories of US involvement and the reclamation of long-silenced experiences of West Indian and other canal laborers from the global majority, the work of uniting these efforts from an environmental perspective remains incomplete.

TRANSNATIONAL ECOWOMANISM
AS A DECOLONIZING FORCE

Womanist scholarship, within the study of religion, emerged out of the contexts of US chattel slavery and the Black Church through the literary mind of Alice Walker and the scholarship of Katie Cannon. Cannon, as part of a small and powerful cohort of emerging Black women scholars at Union Theological Seminary in New York City, gave a lasting name to liberation ethics centered on Black women's lived experiences of race, gender, and class oppression.[4] Her threefold analysis of the need to dismantle structures of oppression in order to center Black women's full humanity in the religious enterprise continues to shape womanist scholarship today. Yet the work of countermemory offers a fourth primary site of analysis for womanist study. One of Cannon's classmates at Union Theological Seminary, womanist theologian Jacquelyn Grant, engaged in related efforts to return Black women's wisdom to a religious scholarship at the time. Grant's writing in 1982, before Cannon's discipline-defining use of the term *womanism*, clearly shows collaborative thinking in the construction of an emerging methodological approach to ethics, biblical studies, and theology.

The work of countermemory in this instance invites the restoration of a fourfold interpretive lens that articulates the primary sites of oppression in need of a womanist methodology. Grant, in her contribution to *Theology in the Americas: Detroit II Conference Papers*, offers an investigation of the tasks of a prophetic church that clearly follows the logics of womanist thought without yet naming it as such. It is from her exploration of the internal work of the prophetic church that we can reclaim a fourfold foundation for womanist study. This evolution lives in the impact of dialogue with women from the two-thirds world on Grant's scholarship. She writes:

> The perspective represented by the various groups of liberation theologians here are not without limitations themselves; for example it reflects special problems for black and other Third World women. Let me use my perspective as a black woman to make the point. My reality is such that I am grounded in the black experience, informed by the feminist analysis, and dedicated to class analysis.

My reading of the tensions which exist among us (liberation theological perspectives) is an attempt to discover where I am. As a black woman, racism, sexism, and classism impinge upon and in fact largely define my existence. Therefore, the analysis of the problem of oppression and the methodology of solution are not academic issues for me, but they bear upon my existential situation.[5]

Grant begins her writing with the threefold interrogation of race, gender, and class oppression that characterizes most of womanist scholarship. But she concludes her paper with clarity that Black women from the United States and from the two-thirds world have a unique authority born of their lived experiences to demand a holistic analysis that calls prophetic churches to engage in the work of self-criticism.[6] She insists that there be room enough to acknowledge the full impact of oppression on Black women from both Global North and Global South, and calls for an alliance with enough strength to birth a true liberation. Grant closes her paper with a visionary claim: "It is the prophetic church that will create the new church—an egalitarian church free of racism / sexism / classism / imperialism, a church which is God's Kingdom on earth."[7]

Grant's foresight invites the addition of anti-imperialism (or a decolonial analysis) to the basic framework of womanist scholarship. This critical expansion acknowledges that the vast majority of peoples forcibly removed from the continent of Africa during the triangle trade never arrived at the continental United States. Grant's prophetic vision echoes Walker's definition of a womanist that includes being "committed to survival and wholeness of entire people . . . traditionally a universalist."[8] The embrace of African diaspora in its fullness and richly diverse complexity is vital for ecowomanist work, not only for reasons of integrity in centering the full humanity of our peoples but also because of the ways in which life on the lands and waters of the African continent and those surrounding or within the Caribbean Sea faces particular dangers in the wake of climate disruption. Ecowomanism must therefore be transnational, decolonial, and deeply informed by an awareness of diaspora.

TERRA NULLIUS AND FERAE BESTIAE

Any consideration of environmental ethics in a transnational womanist frame must engage the disastrous legacies of the philosophical and legal concept of terra nullius. This notion of "empty land" or "no one's land" draws standards of labor, property, and usefulness from natural law to claim the so-called proper utilization of natural resources as a justification for control over foreign, resource-rich territories. While primarily associated with the colonial expansionism of European nations, terra nullius as an ideology fed into American concepts of manifest destiny as a validation of land annexation to the western border of what is now the continental United States.[9] Once that land was completely overrun, "destiny" called US expansionists across the seas. Terra nullius gained its primary notoriety as a legal justification of British dispossession of Aboriginal and Torres Strait Island peoples in what was to become Australia in the late eighteenth century. Yet recent scholarship denounces such attribution as anachronistic historical fiction while still acknowledging the importance of terra nullius as a mindset influencing transnational legal systems over time.[10]

Historian Andrew Fitzmaurice traces the intellectual history of terra nullius, documenting its emergence as an influential philosophy that entered the public eye through the writings of international jurist Camille Piccioni in 1909. Amidst a drawn-out battle over the sovereignty of the polar regions of Earth, Piccioni describes an island under dispute as both terra nullius and a "territory which still has no master."[11] After his publication of this widely read description of a region as one whose relatively small population, lack of resource exploitation, and low property levels negated any sovereignty to which it might otherwise be entitled, discussions of international law regularly cited terra nullius in debates over colonization and the annexation of land.[12] It is important that the language of enslavement is used here to make a moral claim on Earth itself.

As environmental philosopher Deane Curtin asks, "How can public land, owned by no one, be transformed morally into private property?"[13] The answer is to assign virtue to a particular type of relatedness to the land: putting natural resources to their presumed ideal use through the extensive creation of property. That property implies sovereignty, which in turn reaffirms humanity itself.[14] Any peoples or nations that do not submit to such standards are thereby defined as unworthy of their own inherited environmental cultures and relationship to the land. The imperialist gaze wipes such supposedly immoral and uncivilized bodies off of the desired landscape, leaving behind an imagined untrammeled wilderness ripe for the plucking. Invisibilized bodies, now reduced in the moral hierarchy to the status of nonhuman nature, are thereby made available for annexation and control.[15]

Such dehumanization via justifications of exploitative land use provides a vital point of accountability for ecowomanist ethics. Fitzmaurice offers a troubling history of the emergence of terra nullius from its frequently cited roots in the Roman law doctrine of res nullius (no one's property). Terra nullius does not exist in the historical record; instead, the term nullius (definitively no one's) first entered into Roman law through ferae bestiae, "literally the law of wild beasts."[16] In this legislation, the "first taker" of any object, said item being defined as nullius (no one's), is entitled to claim that object as their personal property. The example cited in Roman law is the first person to capture an animal on land, sea, or air.[17] The application of pejorative "bestial" labels to women of African descent for more than five centuries as justification for unscrupulously annihilating acts of violence, deprecation, and control more than justifies interrogating ferae bestiae as a text of terror.[18] Nonhuman nature is denuded of agency unless enslaved in the ideologies of ferae bestiae, terra nullius, or under Roman law. Without a master, lands (and later peoples) are defined as empty, rendering them devoid of both significance and value. There are records of the Portuguese referring to African peoples as dogs as early as the late fifteenth century.[19] This half-millennium association brands Black women and nonhuman animals as beings lacking agency and worth. We ignore the roots of such stereotypes in the seat of Western empire at our peril.

The foundation of womanist ethics is born in part from efforts to resacralize Black women's bodies from the violation of this long and bloody association. In her prophetic, trailblazing text *Black Womanist Ethics*, Katie Cannon draws on the writings of Zora Neale Hurston to construct womanist ethics out of the lived moral wisdom of Black women in their own societal contexts. Hurston's famous description of this bestial correlation is found in the second chapter of *Their Eyes Were Watching God* when Nanny, characteristically passing between generations the wisdom that promotes survival, tells her granddaughter Janie:

> Honey, de white man is de ruler of everything as fur as Ah been able tuh find out. Maybe it's some place way off in de ocean where de black man is in power, but we don't know nothin' but what we see. So de white man throw down de load and tell de nigger man tuh pick it up. He pick it up because he have to, but he don't tote it. He hand it to his womenfolks. De nigger woman is de mule uh de world so fur as Ah can see.

In defining the historical moral context for her construction of womanist ethics, Cannon interrogates "the black woman as 'brood-sow'" and "the black woman as 'work-ox.'"[20] It is appropriate that all of these images interrogate racist imaginaries depicting Black women as laboring farm animals. As the discourse of womanist ethics expands to include ecowomanist perspectives, we must allow a communal association of suffering with nonhuman animals to galvanize our understanding of liberation as something that is shared with all of creation.

TROPICAL TRIUMPHALISM AND THE JUNGLES OF PANAMÁ

Writers communicated "America's Triumph at Panama" during the initial US phase of construction of the Panamá Canal (1904–1914) through easily recognizable tropes of lush, exotic landscapes, as well as the tireless battle against a harsh environment and the moral laxity that it supposedly inspired.[21] These well-worn imaginings were established over the course of the nineteenth century and provided rich material for the emergence of tropical triumphalism during the time of canal construction. Geographer Stephen Frenkel posits that a binary American imaginary characterizing "the tropics" evolved during the nineteenth century based on personal experience and the popular published reflections of those who wrote of their travels. Positive narratives emphasized beauty and wonder to depict an Edenic paradise of rich, productive land, while negative narratives emphasized moral failings, dangerous wilderness, and disease. This dualistic binary did not just capture the American imagination, it also impacted US policies of the time.[22]

Frenkel insists that while overarching conceptions of what was meant by "tropical" already existed, as influenced by the particular moment in history, archetypical depictions also influenced conceptualizations of specific regions. The South Pacific was seen as paradisiacal and western Africa as little more than deadly, but Central America remained less absolute in the American imaginary with elements of both extreme tropical visions present. In general, the tropics of Central America were most commonly depicted to US audiences as "distant paradises or fever coasts" throughout the nineteenth century, though heat and humidity were constants in the popular narrative. The binary's boundaries defined those climatic tendencies as part of the moral landscape. This American imaginary drew its metaphors from limited sources—primarily newspapers, traveler's accounts, and art.[23] At the turn of the century, Panamá, by virtue of its pervasive presence in US art, business, military enterprise, literature, and popular travel accounts, soon became the hegemonic center of an American tropical imaginary.[24]

While Panamá fell neatly into the already established dangerous, disease-ridden side of the dualism, environmental tropes soon proved effective in shifting portions of the metanarrative. Uncontrolled (and therefore inherently unproductive and less worthy) depictions of Panamá gave way to the domination of nature described by the "banana republic" trope, increasing the value of the tropics through agricultural productivity. The triumph of the Panamá Canal would soon serve as the capstone on the monument of US sovereignty over the dark wilderness, and launch what Frenkel refers to as "the theme of 'man's domination over nature.'"[25]

Differences between travelers' perspectives and those newly living on the isthmus reinscribed the two halves of the emerging American tropical imaginary. To the visitor, the tropics of Panamá remained Edenic—a return to an essentialized notion of paradise already lost in the American wilderness. Residents, however, were more likely to report the enervating impact of heat, humidity, and disease. Further analysis reveals that the binary would soon evolve to turn along racial lines. Persistent images portrayed an abundant landscape with untapped potential for rapid growth. Yet the fecundity of the land paralleled settlers' assumptions of the presumed laziness and ease of nonwhite peoples indigenous to Panamá, assumed to benefit from a setting whose abundant sustenance required little labor to produce.[26] Productivity without labor was commonly characterized as a moral failing under Christian notions of a productive landscape (see below).[27] Thus Panamá itself emerged as an ideal setting for the morality traditionally tied to ideologies of terra nullius to develop. The moral landscape itself supposedly cried out for a civilized and civilizing intervention as emphasis shifted from a dark, frightening wilderness to a heroic, God-mandated North American quest for victory. Taming the wilderness, ensuring its productivity, and controlling tropical diseases could secure the viability of an emergent American empire.

The successful construction of the Panamá Canal in the wake of a failed effort by the French government provided an ideal backdrop for idealized notions of US superiority in a time when the rights and responsibilities of the American nation-state were under significant debate. Was it right and godly to expand the United States' borders? To whom did control over the transnational wilderness belong? In a time when the annexation of land and environmental control were painted with a rhetoric of heroism and moral uprightness, the United States established an "environmental ideology of tropical triumphalism"[28] used to rationalize the disruption of entire ecological systems in the name of progress.

Paul Sutter, an environmental historian, writes of an American tropical triumphalism where burgeoning images of an emergent US superpower are drafted through tales of technological triumph and racial superiority. The "celebratory rhetoric" that Sutter describes emerges from a sense of victory over the impossible wilderness of Panamá, an ability to literally sanitize and force order onto a landscape that had killed other, lesser imperialist overtures. While Sutter's work focuses on the mosquito storyline, a tale of discovery of the vector of blood-borne diseases, he clearly captures how technological successes are central to tropical triumphalism in the US canal construction narrative.[29] The ability for civil and sanitation engineering prowess to make possible the survival of the white race in the jungles of Central America clearly points to the rhetorical path of technological modernization justifying environmental devastation that historian Lynn White identifies in his foundational work.

As the initial US period of construction of the canal progressed and the American audience grew more familiar with Panamá, more negative perspectives of the Panamanian tropics turned to the narrative of tropical triumphalism. Many of these were couched in the well-worn trope of environmental determinism, as fears of the lasting impact of time in the tropics were on the rise. Vaughan Cornish, in his presentation on the Panamá Canal works to the Royal Geographic Society in 1908, claimed that Indigenous Panamanians and West Indians were naturally immune to yellow fever and that only large groups of nonimmune outsiders were in danger of contracting the disease.[30] This concern was reason enough to question the ability of Anglo-Saxons to labor well in the tropics.[31]

Soon those living in Panamá were cast as subsisting under the constant specter of impending death and disease. The heat and fecundity of the environment were presumed to instill laziness and indolence, moral failings powerful enough to endanger white settlers.[32] The tropics themselves were a force battling the civilizing influence of an outside benevolent paternalism sent to turn the Panamanian wilderness to the good. Rather than erasing Edenic notions of exotically beautiful landscapes and nature's abundance, the negative fears of darkness, wilderness, and disease shifted to the jungle, a category ripe for disparagement just outside the foothold of order and control that US settlers were placing on Panamá. As Frenkel writes, "If North Americans felt competent to cope with the tropics, they considered the jungle to be out of control."[33] The jungle threatened the narrative of "man's domination over nature," and therefore the justification of growing imperialistic control. A larger intervention was necessary.

There were many triumphs in the tropics of Panamá. US engineers not only succeeded in connecting two oceans for the first time in human history but also their sanitary conquest of the jungle through the near eradication of malaria and yellow fever (accomplished by controlling mosquito populations through control of the land) opened those areas to white male habitation and the acquisition of wealth.[34] The tropics dominated the US environmental narrative of transnational expansion, but what of the racialized and environmentally destructive moral justifications strengthening this imaginary? Conceptualizations of nature and wilderness did not include agency, which Sutter nuances by reminding us that the natural world has moral standing even when its agency cannot be communicated in ways that we understand. He instead labels scientists as actors whose study of the environment renders them capable of interrupting the imperial narrative.[35]

In Sutter's case study, entomologists greatly increased the depth and applicability of their field during the race to eradicate malaria and yellow fever (principal factors contributing to the failure of earlier French efforts to construct an isthmian canal). Entomologists' commitment to the quest for a US victory in Panamá meant that their primary allegiance was to scientific knowledge rather than the environmental imaginary of the time. Sutter writes:

> In Panamá, entomologists worked at a critical juncture between dominant ideas of nature and environmental phenomena; they had intimate experiences with

the material environment that had the potential to reinforce or destabilize ruling ideas of nature and to reveal tensions between their positions and those of other imperial actors. They were not mere captives of tropical ideology.[36]

This proved critical in the mission to lessen disease. US officials primarily focused sanitary efforts on maintaining the health of white workers. They reduced the bodies of nonwhite laborers (primarily West Indians brought to Panamá to work on the canal) to mere vectors of disease, what Sutter describes as a "reservoir of infected people."[37] Entomologists, however, resisted the power of the tropical imaginary by insisting that the racial segregation imposed by US officials was insufficient to eliminate the disease. Instead, following the results of their own studies, entomologists in Panamá made equal efforts to lessen mosquito breeding conditions in areas populated by all workers, regardless of race.[38] It is worth noting that it was the disruption of the natural landscape due to canal construction itself that exacerbated conditions conducive to the increase of the mosquito species primarily responsible for the spread of blood-borne diseases.[39]

Environmental determinism, with its particular popularity during the United States' initial years of canal construction, sanitized otherwise unacceptable positions on race and culture in Panamá. Imported West Indian laborers were assigned the same "tropicality" as Indigenous Panamanians and dehumanized as a morally lax, unsanitary element endangering the health and well-being of white workers. In his article exploring the interconnections between geography, environmental determinism, and the construction of American empire in Panamá, Frenkel notes that racist assumptions harbored within the teachings of environmental determinism gained acceptance where others were denounced. Authorities banned monthly Ku Klux Klan meetings from the Canal Zone because of their destructive impact on certain residents and laborers, while the palliative of social science perspectives on race, culture, and the environment justified similarly harmful stereotypes.[40]

Racist stereotypes further created a paradox about suitability for labor. As Frenkel notes, people of European ancestry were cast as strong, intelligent, efficient, capable, and committed in their labor. The tropes of laziness and stupidity attributed to Indigenous Panamanians and West Indians undermined the call for primary reliance on their labor to build the canal. Environmental determinism neatly unravels this paradox with the claim that whites are climatically unsuited to labor in the tropics, thereby maintaining their place in the hierarchy while relieving them of strenuous work responsibilities.[41]

Stereotypes drawn from environmental and geographic assumptions of people of African descent living in the tropics ranged from the prevalence and spread of disease, to darkness of skin, to an inability to achieve technological successes, to allegedly exotic and strange differences in language and food, to their inherent suitability for labor in the heat. These tropes are unsurprising given the historic proximity to necessary justifications of chattel slavery across the Caribbean and the US South. As Frenkel notes, "These beliefs were assumed to be scientifically valid and *morally neutral* [emphasis mine], because influence on humans was an empirically proven fact."[42] The power of science transformed otherwise corrupt ideas (as seen by the rejection of the KKK's presence in the Canal Zone) into everyday knowledge and common sense. The environment of Panamá thereby became not only a proving ground for American dominion, but also the silenced agent whose imagined voice legitimized imperial control.

In Panamá, the ability of science to interrupt imperial tropes proved to be time limited. Sutter notes that entomologists, who in many ways defied the standard narrative by focusing on vector control rather than imperial priorities and blame based on stereotyped images of race and sanitation, swiftly returned to tropical triumphalism after the completion of the canal. The field of entomology blossomed as part of the rhetoric of subjugating the wilderness to allow for white settlement and economic growth. The disease narrative became one of American triumph over mosquitoes and squalor rather than one of repairing human-induced environmental devastation.[43] A rhetoric celebrating control over wild lands and "primitive" peoples added moral justification to the conquest of both.

The validation of imperialism on moral grounds interrupted the accepted US approach to foreign policy at the time, which shied away from anything reminiscent of European colonialism. Treaties defined appropriate relations with other nations to the assumed benefit of both parties.[44] Yet the ability to build a canal across the Isthmus of Panamá offered the possibility of simplified travel and a maneuverable navy, both highly valuable at the time.[45] Moral rationalization became a primary concern in the face of such contradictions. In the words of historian Julie Greene, "In its triumph, the Panama Canal articulated American expansionism as a positive, humane, and beneficial activity, one equally valuable to world civilization and to American national identity."[46] While US officials were careful to never fully annex Panamá as a colony, limiting their official governance and control by treaty to the area that eventually became the Canal Zone, the continued call of manifest destiny loomed large in debates over the expansion of US international interests.[47]

Manifest destiny, like notions of the tropics, encountered Central America in the American imaginary through the writings of travelers.[48] Its malleability as an ideology allowed expansionists to critique European colonization while simultaneously dreaming of an expansive, transnationally influential United States.[49] With roots in Protestant visions of American culture serving as a moral exemplar for the supposedly less civilized world, manifest destiny offered absolution from otherwise immoral acts of conquest. The power of this imaginary can be seen in the debates over the righteousness of an expansionist approach. In his six-book history tracing the debates over US expansion, Murat Halstead describes the sovereignty of two tropical nations as

> elaborate pretenses of government constructed for speculative purposes or experiments in local and native tyranny, by those who as insurgents were enabled to hide their public character in the swamps and thickets of tropical forests until liberated by our triumphant arms.[50]

His treatise, published in 1899, emphasizes the larger duty of those who would liberate the less fortunate, even by force. He proclaims, "Every drop of the blood of our countrymen so shed seals an everlasting covenant of our dominion over the soil that it sanctifies."[51] The moral context of his position could not be clearer.

Halstead establishes the context of his moral claims in pointed environmental terms. His *Pictorial History of America's New Possessions: The Isthmian Canals and the Problem of Expansion* opens with images of American forefathers, the white men that Halstead felt had accomplished the most in expanding US influence and imperial possessions. The inscription of this catalog of moral priorities is laden with religious imagery defined by an environmental manifest destiny.

Inscribed:
To the farmer fathers of the Republic of the United States,
the expanders of our Dominions with Right and Might,
Compelling Civilization with the axe, the rifle, and the plow,
moving west the center of population of the glorious nation
in the course the poet prophets
marked on the soil and in the sky
for the stars of empire, giving Oceans for boundaries
of the land provided for their children
With the policy of new possessions beyond the seas
Including the treasure islands
Of all the zones of the northern hemisphere
For all the people of all the states
According to the logic of history
And the duty of destiny.[52]

Halstead's entire six-book offering traces US expansion outside of its continental borders to catalog debates on the feasibility and moral uprightness of constructing an isthmian canal. It is clear from his opening words that such effort rests on logics of tropical triumphalism.

In Panamá the United States offered "civilization" in exchange for immense natural resources, strategic military positioning, transnational shipping and its profits, and political control. None of these would be morally plausible unless those already occupying the landscape (human agents robbed of voice) could be depicted as incapable of producing what the very landscape itself (a nonhuman agent also robbed of voice) cried out to become. By calling US intervention and progress a "mandate from civilization," as President Theodore Roosevelt claimed while arguing to construct the canal before Congress in 1904, "an American presence could be framed in an ostensibly scientific discourse without raising the sensitive issue of imperialism."[53] Roosevelt explicitly chose morality to validate aggressive US treaty negotiations establishing complete US control over the Canal Zone. Civilization stood on its own as a moral justification. Roosevelt never established the authority of such a mandate.[54]

Stephen Frenkel's exhaustive corpus detailing the impact of environmental determinism and tropical triumphalism as American imaginaries used to justify US quasi-colonialism in Panamá and other parts of the world evolved over the course of his career to include a cogent analysis of otherization. By 2002 his writing notes the prevalent silencing of all agents in the narrative that do not qualify as white US residents. He explains that US whites categorized Panamá as a whole as Other, an ostracism that silenced all priorities, rights, and needs outside of their own. As expected, West Indians and Indigenous Panamanians (slandered by the aforementioned stereotypes of laziness, indolence, and harboring disease) as well as wilderness and poorly cultivated landscapes (both considered dangerous to the white American settler) were used to justify economic and political privileges for the dominant group.[55] He insists that "'Othering' narratives and ideologies guided American organization and development of the Zone, providing the legitimizing means by which to formulate policies, subjugate people, and create an American suburb in the tropics."[56] While Frenkel's work has grown more pointed over time, and his willingness to connect abject racism with environmental tropes has gained clarity, he has not gone so far as to attempt to rectify the silencing of the Otherness that he considers so effective in supporting American imperialism in Panamá. There remains a profound need to hear the voices of other actors in the narratives he describes.

Tropical tropes shaped American understandings of multiple silenced agents in the Panamanian landscape: populations of Indigenous Panamanians that fall outside the scope of this inquiry, West Indian migrants, women whose presence regardless of race is barely documented in the historical record, and the environment itself. Frenkel makes clear from the standpoint of geography that popular depictions of Panamá's wilderness clearly justified US imperialism and dominance in the region. His exploration of tropical tropes also acknowledges the primary lack of nonwhite, non-North American voices in its description.[57] These lived experiences, reduced by white settlers to the jungle side of the binary, offer new ground in reconsidering a moral landscape. To recover those voices, to return agency to those who labored within the confines of the American transnational environmental imaginary, is to sift through the sanitizing imaginings of a society bent on domestication and control.

SEX WORK IN THE PORNO-TROPICS: "THE MORALS OF ALL THE WOMEN IN CAMP ARE GOOD"

So-called jungle stories were clearly in evidence when the steamship Floridian arrived at Colon in early November 1905 carrying an estimated 650 migrants from Martinique.[58] For the first time during the US period of canal construction, a large number of women of African descent arrived in Panamá as a noticeable group.[59] Approximately 280 Black women disembarked from the Floridian, their passages paid by the United States as part of an effort to recruit and retain the labor of Martiniquan men.[60] Their arrival sparked immediate controversy bolstered by rumors that they were brought to Panamá for purposes of prostitution.

There is no question that sex work existed, and was eventually even regulated, in areas just outside the Canal Zone. White canal workers and West Indian laborers both include the reality of prostitution in written recollections of construction days.[61] What is notable about this sequence of events is that the appearance of a large group of dark-skinned women immediately generated outcries against not only their presumed immorality but also indecency on the part of the United States for bringing them in the first place. Protests arose in response to a narrative that threatened the sanitized American story of empire, one that replaced resource theft and land annexation with the language of civilization, morality, and faithfulness. Sex work itself is not immoral, though it would have frequently been disparaged as such in the American language of the early twentieth century. What was at stake in the debate was the plausibility of benevolence in US foreign expansions.

In this instance, two powerful tropes struggle for dominance over the Black woman's body. By this point in history the American imaginary is well versed in stereotypes of women of African descent as defined by a negative view of nature—wild to the point of bestial with concomitant insatiable sexual appetites. It is no stretch for white Americans to equate the newly arrived Black woman's body with a hypersexualized, uncontrollable Panamanian jungle. Yet the American imaginary also sought to define itself as the righteous force of civilization, destined to liberate lesser humans from their "primitive" state.

Unsurprisingly, it was what feminist literary scholar Anne McClintock names the "porno-tropic tradition" that controlled the story in the public eye.[62]

The language of the porno-tropics neatly exposes a master narrative that first defines Black women's sexuality as inherently immoral and then seeks to save Black women from themselves by controlling every aspect of their existence—from their bodies, values, and labor to the very land they occupy. McClintock describes the porno-tropics as "a fantastic magic lantern of the mind onto which Europe projected its forbidden sexual desires and fears."[63] Long before the era of European expansionism, eroticized narratives of the depravity of foreign lands captivated the European imagination through images of dark-skinned women copulating with baboons and awaiting, lustfully, the attentions of European men.[64] These narratives, which became central to European colonizing efforts, entered the American imagination during the American colonial period. Further reinforced by the logics of chattel slavery, the recurring tropes of the porno-tropics are documented by anthropologists studying white expatriate masculinities to this day.[65] It is not difficult to understand why rumors of prostitution followed the arrival of almost three hundred women from Martinique like wildfire.

It is important to note that outside of recent histories intentionally aimed at reconstructing the overlooked experiences of West Indian communities, and West Indian women in particular, during the construction of the Panamá Canal, few historians describe West Indian women in the early 1900s as anything other than prostitutes. Some briefly acknowledge their work as domestics, but the lasting and defining image of West Indian women in the historiography is one of prostitution. It is therefore critical to begin the work of ecowomanist ethics at the site of the Panamá Canal with this story. US officials insisted that the Martiniquan women were brought to Panamá to support their husbands or to work as cooks, laundresses, and maids. A letter from Chief Engineer John F. Stevens to T. P. Shonts, chair of the Isthmian Canal Commission, supports part of this assertion. On December 14, 1905, Stevens wrote to Shonts to report on labor shortages at the construction sites. The attrition of laborers over time was greater than expected and Stevens was in need of five thousand workers. His letter explains that the Jamaican government was blocking US recruiters and the Chinese government planned to do the same. He intends to send agents to Cartagena and Martinique, but worries that efforts to recruit Martiniquan laborers will ultimately fail. He writes,

> I do not think we can do much at Martinique, as the men flatly refuse to leave there except they be allowed to bring their women along; and you know what the result would be in case we attempted this. We will do the best we can to find out in all cases whether the women who come along are legal wives, and I presume we cannot afford to take any other risks.[66]

The legality of marriage was of particular importance (see below). Clearly, rumors already limited the choices that US officials felt they could justify.

G. Bonhenry, French vice-consul at Colón, describes the US action as an effort to alleviate the homesickness of Martiniquan laborers, taking pride in the appearance and comportment of Martiniquan women as superior to others from non-French speaking West Indian islands. His earlier letter to the US Department of Foreign Affairs on November 16, 1905, explains that 310 women had arrived from Martinique, from the families of men coming to work on the canal as well as those who were already living on the isthmus. He says that additional women who made the trip were intended to serve as cooks and laundresses. Bonhenry believes this new labor recruitment strategy will "render it easier to attract and retain Martiniquan laborers on the Isthmus. . . . In any event, one can not [*sic*] but praise the spirit of this measure."[67]

Poultney Bigelow soon proved Bonhenry's enthusiasm wrong with an incendiary article that controlled the story. Bigelow was a lawyer and professor of colonial expansion at Boston University.[68] He was a prolific writer known for his study of conditions affecting Black laborers around the world.[69] His January 4, 1906, polemic against government mismanagement and horrific living conditions for West Indian laborers working on the Panamá Canal, "Our Mismanagement at Panama," only contained three paragraphs on the question of prostitution. But the following words outraged the American public:

> On the occasion of my visit the clergy of the Isthmus were loud in protest because the United States authorities had imported at considerable expense several colored ladies. Prostitutes are not needed on the Isthmus—and if they were there is no call to send for them at the expense of the taxpayer.[70]

President Roosevelt sent a message to Congress refuting the charges within days and further critiqued Bigelow for drawing his conclusions from a mere two-day visit to Panamá.[71]

The Independent, which published Bigelow's article, sent two journalists (Edwin Slosson and Gardner Richardson) to Panamá to corroborate his story. They documented inaccuracies in Bigelow's accounts yet never gave a final opinion on the issue of prostitution. Their writings still cast a stereotype of prostitution, confirming that residents of the Canal Zone were certain of the immoral lives of the Martiniquan women. Their statement on women predictably defines them in earthly terms: "The three things lacking to make life enjoyable on the Isthmus are all feminine—women, cows, and hens."[72] Again we find traces of terra nullius in the legitimizing tropes of the American empire.

Bigelow did not repeat his accusations of prostitution—neither during the US Senate's investigation into his charges nor in his reaffirmation of canal work criticisms published in *The New York Times* on January 12, 1906. But his elision of "colored women" and "prostitution" shaped the canal's narrative for over a century. The morality of sex work itself was not openly debated; it was simply assumed to be both sinful and uncivilized. Rather, it was the idea of the US government paying for the migration of women of African descent for the purposes of prostitution that threatened the narrative of US interventions as a civilizing move. Paying for prostitution, for all that white laborers made regular use of the red-light districts outside of the Canal Zone, laid the moral burden back on the United States to prove the moral uprightness of its efforts in Panamá. Better to parade 167 women before a lawyer to make affidavits about their moral character under the assumed threat of deportation. The United States did exactly that.

Charles E. Magoon, governor of the Panamá Canal Zone, makes clear during his testimony before the US Senate Committee on Interoceanic Canals that the purpose of the affidavits collected from 167 Martiniquan women from January 17 through January 19, 1906, was to "show what representations were made to those women in Martinique by our labor agent."[73] Canal Zone attorney J. M. Keedy traveled to the women's places of residence, made his inquiries, and "reduced their statements to the form of an affidavit."[74] Keedy reported to the governor that the women in question were well aware of the attacks on their morality and displayed visible alarm and distress at the thought that they might be forced to return to Martinique. He describes their consistent denial of the charges and clarity that their lifestyles were not sinful. Those who were living with men without legal marital status expressed clear values of monogamy, fidelity, and the intent to marry with respect to their relationships.[75] West Indian communities on the isthmus regularly practiced a type of common-law marriage, encouraged by exorbitant marriage fees from the churches and the government. Magoon emphasized testimony from Rose Mont Rose that she never expected to be working as a prostitute and that she was explicitly told "that I must either be married, have work, or leave the camps, as they wanted no single women here unless they were working."[76]

Two clergy members also testified before the Senate committee, adding their affirmation of the Martiniquan women and refuting Bigelow's claims. Both George Oscar Eskins (an Anglican minister named by Bigelow in his original article who denied that association) and J. L. Wise (a Baptist minister sent as a missionary to Panamá by the Southern Baptist Convention) described the women as moral, law abiding, and hardworking during their two months on the isthmus.[77] Wise affirmed the validity of the common-law marriages and further claimed that the women "conducted themselves in such as manner as to change the bad opinion which was entertained by the public soon after their arrival."[78] This statement is echoed by Caribbean scholar Olive Senior, who traces the perceptions of Martiniquan women from their starting point in scandal, to their survival of character defamation, to their positive role in establishing "multinational, multicultural West Indian families on the Isthmus."[79]

West Indian laborers later spoke of the influx of women from Martinique in reflections collected as part of a competition to document life in the Canal Zone. Harrigan Austin remembers that at the very start of canal construction there were few women and their absence created significant disadvantages and difficulties. He recalls the US government bringing French women from Martinique and that those who wished could take responsibility for one of those women through marriage.[80] Albert Peter remembers problems with basic life necessities in the absence of women. He laments laborers having to bathe, clean, and do laundry all in the same river. Peter jokes that most of the time the men went to work half naked.[81]

While the comprehensive efforts on the part of US officials to quell allegations of prostitution were undertaken to protect the emerging narrative of American tropical triumphalism in the public eye, an unintended benefit of their work is the addition of 167 women from Martinique to the historic record (see appendix A). These voices, whose identities would have otherwise likely been erased into a footnote as "colored women," instead offer small glimpses into their lives during the construction era. Several themes emerge from their affidavits, even redacted as they were by Keedy.

Satisfying US officials' intentions for the affidavits' purpose, many of the women spoke to their recruitment (most often by a Mr. Lavenel) for various types of domestic labor.

Bluempia Messon: "I was informed by Mr. Lavenel that I could get plenty of work here, and I came here for that purpose."[82]

Jane Practrice: "I was informed by the American agent in Martinique that I could come here and join my husband and get plenty of work. . . . The agent was Mr. Lavenel."[83]

Marie Vulnon: "I am single and came here to work, having seen in newspapers that I could get some. I was also told by an American in Martinique the same."[84]

Estafan Lendo: "I was sent here by Mr. Lavenel who promised me work as cook, laundress, etc. at different hotels."[85]

Jane Alfonce: "I was informed by Mr. Lavenel that I could get plenty of work and good wages here, such as washing, cooking, and general housework."[86]

Maria Julia: "I am from Martinique and came here two months and sixteen days ago—myself and sister. The agent at Martinique did not say anything to me. I paid my fare here."[87]

In just two and a half months several of the women or their husbands had already experienced injury, illness, or death from their labors.

Dennis Denir: "Mr. Lavenel got me to come here to better my condition by working and getting good wages, as servants were needed at hotels, hospitals, and private families. I had work until I hurt my hand and am under the care of a doctor. I live in the camp, which is protected all night by watchmen and policemen, and no one is allowed to come there."[88]

Louis Ponalaie: "I was married sixteen years ago in Martinique and came here with my husband, who works on the canal, but is now sick in the hospital."[89]

Finez Willy: "I was married in Martinique about one and one-half years ago and came here to join my husband who came before me. I lived with him until his death. I am now working as cook in a restaurant, and live in said restaurant."[90]

Migration to Panamá was frequently a choice to improve daily life. The vast majority of affidavits expressed satisfaction with the decision.

Zanda Oska: "I am from Martinique, with my husband and three children, the oldest being 18 years. I came here two months and seventeen days ago. The agent told me I would meet her husband and could get work with good wages. My husband and son are both assisting as carpenters, and I am washing, with my daughter, for other laborers. We are doing better here than in Martinique."[91]

Katherine Ernest: "I was told by Mr. Lavenel in Martinique that I could find plenty of work here, and I came for that purpose. I am now working as a laundress. I wash and iron for my living. I came with my husband from Martinique, and live with him at Empire, Canal Zone, and we are both saving money."[92]

Margarete P. Pole: "I can't make as much money in Martinique as I can here, and I like it."[93]

Mrs. Leona Louis: "My husband died about five years ago, and, hearing that there was plenty of work here, came and have been employed ever since. I came here as a house servant in an American Family. I get $20 a month, with accommodation. I sleep with a cousin of mine, but is [sic] promised a room in the family soon. I am well satisfied. No one ever told me I had to have a husband."[94]

Finally, there are a significant number of claims of moral living. Most of these are descriptions of sleeping arrangements, hard work, and marital status. They are perhaps best exemplified in the words of Alfonce Ustach:

I am single, and came here to get work. Have been informed by newspapers and American agent in Martinique that I could get plenty of work and good wages here. I am working now as a washerwoman at the hotel in Culebra, and my treatment and wages are all right, and I don't want to leave. I live in camp with other single

Martinique women, and a watchman is over us all night, who allows no one to leave or enter our quarters after 8:30 p.m. I am 69 years old. The morals of all the women in camp are good. They work hard during the day and retire early at night.[95]

While I contend that pervasive ideologies aligning Black women's bodies with a bestial hypersexuality are so firmly interwoven into the American imaginary as to transcend national borders, it is important to consider the multiple displacements of the women in question. Their inherited environmental cultures (see chapter 1) are transmitted via the forced displacement of enslavement to embrace a West Indian identity and then again through the chosen displacement of migration driven by the need for work opportunities, family, and various forms of independence. An ecowomanist ethic shaped by questions of ecocreolization must therefore consider the coconstruction of race, class, gender, and inherited environmental cultures. This fourfold identity formation lays the foundation for an ecowomanist moral anthropology.

NOTES

1. For a description of a Protestant "ethic of control" see Sharon D. Welch, *A Feminist Ethic of Risk*, rev. ed. (Minneapolis: Fortress Press, 2000), 25, 49, 104.

2. Julie Greene, *The Canal Builders: Making America's Empire at the Panama Canal* (New York: Penguin Books, 2009), 9.

3. Greene, *Canal Builders*, 10.

4. Cannon, *Katie's Canon*, 136–40.

5. Jacquelyn Grant, "Tasks of a Prophetic Church," in *Theology in the Americas: Detroit II Conference Papers*, ed. Cornel West, Caridad Guidote, and Margaret Coakley (Maryknoll, NY: Orbis Books, 1982), 138.

6. Grant, "Tasks of a Prophetic Church," 139.

7. Grant, "Tasks of a Prophetic Church," 141–42.

8. For Alice Walker's catalytic definition of a womanist, see Alice Walker, *In Search of Our Mothers' Gardens: Womanist Prose* (San Diego: Harcourt Brace Jovanovich, 1983), xi–xii.

9. Deane Curtin, *Environmental Ethics for a Postcolonial World* (Lanham, MD: Rowman & Littlefield, 2005), 3–4.

10. Andrew Fitzmaurice, "The Genealogy of *Terra Nullius*," *Australian Historical Studies* 38, no. 129 (2007): 2. https://doi.org/10.1080/10314610708601228.

11. Fitzmaurice, "Genealogy of *Terra Nullius*," 3–4.

12. Fitzmaurice, "Genealogy of *Terra Nullius*," 3–4.

13. Curtin, *Environmental Ethics*, 3–4.

14. Fitzmaurice, "Genealogy of *Terra Nullius*," 13.

15. Plumwood, *Environmental Culture*, 104.

16. Fitzmaurice, "Genealogy of *Terra Nullius*," 6.

17. Fitzmaurice, "Genealogy of *Terra Nullius*," 6.

18. Phillis Tribble coined the term *text of terror* in her landmark text *Texts of Terror: Literary-Feminist Readings of Biblical Narratives* (Philadelphia: Fortress Press, 1984).

19. For further exploration of bestial labels used to belittle both Black women and nonhuman animals, see Kwaku Osei-Tutu, "Growth of the Atlantic Slave Trade: Racial Slavery in the New World," in *Color Struck: Essays on Race and Ethnicity in Global Perspective*, ed. Julius O. Adekunle and Hettie V. Williams (Lanham, MD: University Press of America, 2012), 93–112.

20. Katie G. Cannon, *Black Womanist Ethics* (Atlanta: Scholars Press, 1988), 32–33.

21. "America's Triumph at Panama" is the title of a popular 1913 text by Ralph Emmett Avery.

22. Stephen Frenkel, "Jungle Stories: North American Representations of Tropical Panama," *Geographic Review* 86, no. 3 (July 1996): 317–18.

23. Frenkel, "Jungle Stories," 318–19.

24. Frenkel, "Jungle Stories," 321.

25. Frenkel, "Jungle Stories," 320–21.

26. Frenkel, "Jungle Stories," 323–24.

27. Whitney Bauman, *Theology, Creation, and Environmental Ethics: From Creatio Ex Nihilo to Terra Nullius* (New York: Routledge, 2009), 58.

28. Paul Sutter, "Nature's Agents or Agents of Empire? Entomological Workers and Environmental Change during the Construction of the Panama Canal," *Isis* 98, no. 4 (December 2007): 726, https://doi.org/10.1086/529265.

29. Sutter, "Nature's Agents," 725.

30. Cornish, "Panama Canal," 154.

31. Cornish, "Panama Canal," 171–72.

32. Frenkel, "Jungle Stories," 325–26.

33. Frenkel, "Jungle Stories," 327.

34. Sutter, "Nature's Agents," 725.

35. Sutter, "Nature's Agents," 728–29.

36. Sutter, "Nature's Agents," 729.

37. Sutter, "Nature's Agents," 733.

38. Sutter, "Nature's Agents," 747–48, 752.

39. Sutter, "Nature's Agents," 740–41, 744.

40. Stephen Frenkel, "Geography, Empire, and Environmental Determinism," *Geographical Review* 82, no. 2 (April 1992): 144, https://doi.org/10.2307/215428.

41. Frenkel, "Geography, Empire," 149.

42. Frenkel, "Geography, Empire," 144–45.

43. Sutter, "Nature's Agents," 753–54.

44. Frenkel, "Geography, Empire," 144–45.

45. Greene, *Canal Builders*, 350–51.

46. Greene, *Canal Builders*, 9.

47. Frenkel, "Geography, Empire," 145–46.

48. Amy S. Greenberg, *Manifest Manhood and the Antebellum American Empire* (Cambridge: Cambridge University Press, 2005), 78.

49. Greenberg, *Manifest Manhood*, 19–20.

50. Murat Halstead, *Pictorial History of America's New Possessions: The Isthmian Canals and the Problem of Expansion* (Chicago: W.S. Reeve, 1899), 11.

51. Halstead, *Pictorial History*, 11.

52. Halstead, *Pictorial History*, front matter.

53. Frenkel, "Geography, Empire," 146.

54. Walter LaFeber, *The Panama Canal: The Crisis in Historical Perspective* (New York: Oxford University Press, 1978), 40.

55. Stephen Frenkel, "Geographical Representations of the 'Other': The Landscape of the Panama Canal Zone," *Journal of Historical Geography* 28, no. 1 (2002): 96, https://doi.org/10.1006/jhge.2001.0375.

56. Frenkel, "Geographical Representations," 86.

57. Frenkel, "Jungle Stories," 321.

58. *Investigation of Panama Canal Matters: Hearings before the Committee on Interoceanic Canals of the United States Senate in the Matter of the Senate Resolution Adopted January 9, 1906, Providing for an Investigation of Matters Relating to the Panama Canal, Etc.*, vols. 1–4 (Washington, DC: Government Printing Office, 1907), 936.

59. David McCullough, *The Path between the Seas: The Creation of the Panama Canal 1870–1914* (New York: Simon & Schuster, 1977), 577.

60. *Investigation of Panama Canal Matters*, 859, 936.

61. Eyra Marcela Reyes Rivas, *El trabajo de las mujeres en la historia de la Construcción del Canal de Panamá 1881–1914* (Panamá City: Universidad de Panamá Instituto de la Mujer, 2000), 148–50.

62. Anne McClintock, *Imperial Leather: Race, Gender, and Sexuality in the Colonial Context* (New York: Routledge, 1995), 22.

63. McClintock, *Imperial Leather*, 22.

64. McClintock, *Imperial Leather*, 22–23.

65. Kelly Brown Douglas, *Sexuality and the Black Church* (New York: Orbis Books, 1999), 32–33; Thomas Hendricks, "Race and Desire in the Porno-Tropics: Ethnographic Perspectives from the Post-colony," *Sexualities* 17, nos. 1–2 (2014): 217, 218, https://doi.org/10.1177/1363460713511100.

66. J. F. Stevens to T. P. Shonts, December 14, 1905, George Westerman Collection (MG505 48/19), Schomburg Center for Research in Black Culture, New York Public Library.

67. *Investigation of Panama Canal Matters*, 859.

68. Greene, *Canal Builders*, 195.

69. Poultney Bigelow, "Our Mismanagement at Panama," *Independent*, January 4, 1906, reprinted in *Message from the President of the United States Transmitting Certain Papers to Accompany His Message of January 8, 1906* (Washington, DC: Government Publishing Office, 1906), 79.

70. Bigelow, "Our Mismanagement at Panama," 90.

71. Greene, *Canal Builders*, 196–98.

72. Greene, *Canal Builders*, 196–98.

73. *Investigation of Panama Canal Matters*, 842.

74. *Investigation of Panama Canal Matters*, 932.
75. *Investigation of Panama Canal Matters*, 932.
76. *Investigation of Panama Canal Matters*, 842.
77. *Investigation of Panama Canal Matters*, 933, 937–38.
78. *Investigation of Panama Canal Matters*, 938.
79. Senior, *Dying to Better Themselves*, 252–53.
80. Rivas, *El trabajo de las mujeres,* 143–44.
81. Rivas, *El trabajo de las mujeres,* 143–44.
82. *Investigation of Panama Canal Matters*, 967.
83. *Investigation of Panama Canal Matters*, 970.
84. *Investigation of Panama Canal Matters*, 965.
85. *Investigation of Panama Canal Matters*, 948.
86. *Investigation of Panama Canal Matters*, 970.
87. *Investigation of Panama Canal Matters*, 949.
88. *Investigation of Panama Canal Matters*, 947.
89. *Investigation of Panama Canal Matters*, 967.
90. *Investigation of Panama Canal Matters*, 974.
91. *Investigation of Panama Canal Matters*, 955.
92. *Investigation of Panama Canal Matters*, 971.
93. *Investigation of Panama Canal Matters*, 965.
94. *Investigation of Panama Canal Matters*, 979.
95. *Investigation of Panama Canal Matters*, 960.

Chapter 3

The Silver Sisters

Ecocreolization at the Panamá Canal

Ecocreolization is an agential response to the slow violence of neo-imperialism and forced displacement/migration. It is the process of self-definition and meaning making that arises in response to interrelated violence centered on race, class, gender, and the environment. Ecocreolization insists that the formation of African diasporic identities and cultures cannot be fully understood without engaging our relationship to Earth. Through coconstructions of race, class, gender, and the natural world, ecocreolization reveals what it means to be fully human in a time of climate disruption. Some might not consider the trip to work at the site of the Panamá Canal an example of forced migration, yet the conditions that pushed so many West Indians to make the journey serve to collectively remove agency from those driven by a need to survive. While West Indian stories are largely missing from the historical record, the work of several scholars seeks to repair the silence surrounding the contributions of Caribbean migrants to the construction of the Panamá Canal. Panamá itself is recasting the tale of Black male laborers, primarily from Barbados and Jamaica, as heroes of the nation. Yet the histories and contributions of Black women, the silver sisters, remain almost absent from the archives and records in both the United States and Panamá.[1] In order to construct an ecowomanist ethic in connection with the Panamá Canal, it is necessary to reclaim and incorporate the inherited environmental teachings of women who migrated to labor in a wide variety of ways. There are echoes in the historical record, memories captured mainly through the dehumanizing writings of white men and women, that diversify the frequent US categorization of West Indian women at the canal as sex workers imported for the "morale" of male laborers (see chapter 2). There is also a shadow archive, a collection of family memories, artifacts, and songs—an insistence, particularly among the female descendants of those laboring women, to make their voices heard. That shadow archive provides one more opportunity to "mine the motherload," as womanist theoethicist Stacey Floyd-Thomas would say, and reclaim the cultural inheritance of our mothers' knowings.

The archival records are replete with examples of governmental proceedings, engineering advances, and a self-congratulatory American triumph over the natural barriers of wilderness that defeated the French. The plight of the West Indian worker is captured through the lens of the white gaze mostly in romanticized, vainglorious writing most particularly by white women living in the Canal Zone as their husbands worked on behalf of the US neo-imperialism. These women saw themselves in the "hard times" of the dark laborer, stranded as they were in the jungle wilds with only one another and their correspondence as remnants of the supposed civilization they clung to desperately. Back "home," Americans consumed travel memoirs and insider reports on the realities of canal life—particularly those with a white savior bent—with a delight we might presently reserve for romance novels and soap operas. How are we to find aspects of identity development from West Indian women's real lived experiences of the time? Many scholars have written extensively on the unequal and brutal treatment that West Indian men experienced as laborers on the canal. Multiple mythographies remain important (see chapter 1), as do insights gained from cultural expressions of the time. While the devaluation of male West Indian laborers is immediately quantifiable through the gold and silver rolls cataloging compensation for work on the canal, the racial and ecological identity development of the West Indian woman is less documented in the historical record. We seek for her presence in memoirs and governmental records. We find her in newspaper clippings and casual observation. Terribly, we find her in the mocking stereotypes used by white American women in their desperate attempts to distance themselves from the hardship and struggle of life in the Canal Zone.

This chapter moves through an arc of depictions of West Indian women not only during the United States' first phase of canal construction from 1904 to 1914 but also in the intermittent years between the canal's completion and its expansion in 1939 when the potential Panamanian citizenship of West Indian laborers was uncertain and tenuous. West Indian women can no longer be stereotyped and dismissed as disparaged sex workers no one wanted to admit were doing real work that was in real demand at the time (see chapter 2). Their range of labor, family structures, and support is hidden in the margins of history. In the early 1900s, when canal labor was scarce and no one wanted to claim the thousands who risked and dedicated their lives digging the big ditch, the easy erasure of human worth and valuation severely impacted West Indian life. This serves as an excellent example of what Rob Nixon terms "displaced in place," when there is nowhere to go, a sense of home is scarce, there is real environmental devastation, and only certain communities are welcome to express their values and priorities in the wake of a major environmental disturbance. A community is further displaced in place when there is a predatory loss of access to land and resources without community relocation.[2]

West Indian laborers and families found themselves displaced in place when the canal no longer wanted them, Panamá refused to claim them as citizens, the already existing Panamanian Black community remaining from sixteenth-century Spanish enslavement felt separate from them due to language and cultural (read: colonized) barriers, and the British empire ironically no longer bore any responsibility for them due to the realities of emancipation. As is characteristic of destructive imperial legacies to this day, no nation wanted to take responsibility for the inheritance of acts of immense environmental devastation. The complexities of knowing oneself through racialization and ecocreolization during the years of canal construction and expansion offer a unique viewpoint into the construction of inherited environmental cultures and their vital role in responding to climate disruption in our own time.

The Canal Zone culture of publishing memoirs and commentaries led to several unsavory depictions of Black women during the time of canal construction. Some were nevertheless grounded in real, existing relationships, no matter how unequal the power of the players, and consequently offer glimpses into the humanity of West Indian domestics, laundresses, market sellers, and others. But more often the record illustrates stereotypes of West Indian women on the canal, observed spitefully from afar or, worse, lumped into dehumanizing categories by those unwilling and unable to acknowledge their dependence on the knowledge of West Indian women as the survival-seeking centers of the family and the community. Ingenious, industrious, and good at surviving—this is how women in my own extended family describe the West Indian community (see "Reaping the Sweets"). There is an unbending pride in a sense of self that is inherited from those who lived in such times. In their wisdom, they identified those of us descended from canal laborers as the ones who reap the sweetness of the fruit planted in those days. We are the literal inheritors of environmental culture and a valuation of self. We are the embodiment of stories told in environmental time. To understand such knowing as an invaluable resource, we must begin with depictions from others' distasteful views, while offering heart-broken open apologies to those ancestors whose glory is diminished in such vile materials.

MACWALBAX AND THE DOGGERELIZATION OF THE WEST INDIAN WOMAN IN PANAMÁ

An advertisement on the front inside cover of *Macwalbax: A Collection of Poems, Cartoons, and Comment* describes *The Panama American* (a daily

Panamanian American newspaper) as a publication that "owes no obligation to any set, group, clique or crown, political, religious, economic or commercial."[3] The ad identifies *The Panama American* as having "an individuality and a personal opinion that it is not afraid to express. Thousands like it, thousands hate it—but everybody reads it."[4] The *daily paper* was published by the Panama Times Ltd. publishers in the Canal Zone starting in 1925. This publishing company, owned by Nelson Rounsevell and renamed The Panama American Publishing Company in 1927 after heroic efforts by readers to resurrect the daily serial once debts from high operational costs forced its suspension earlier that year, disseminated a range of opinion-driven materials characterized as humorous, biting, or influential to Americans in the Canal Zone.[5] It circulated a very specific type of observations of life at the site of the Panamá Canal, including the *daily paper*, a weekly serial circulated alongside the Sunday edition of *The Panama American* that also bore the name *The Panama Times* and the books *Isthmiana* and *Macwalbax*, among others.

John K. Baxter, editor of *The Panama American* and contributor to *Macwalbax*, characterized himself as an "arch enemy of hokum, Nemesis of fakes, rum highball adept, Harvard graduate, author of 'Pro and Con, Mostly Con,' and editor of The Panama American."[6] He goes on to say of himself that

> his pen wields a stronger influence on Isthmian affairs than that of any other writer and he holds the daily attention and admiration of a large circle of readers. . . . To be a guest at the frequent gatherings in his "Cellular Bungalow" is counted as a privilege.[7]

Rounsevell referred to Baxter as his "star feature writer," having agreed to publish "anything and everything that he had the nerve to sign."[8] This carte blanche approach caused significant trouble for the paper, resulting in a contentious meeting with the president of Panamá in its first month of publication.[9] Yet Rounsevell also credits Baxter as the voice that brought recognition to the Panama Times as a publisher at a time that no others had succeeded in establishing a prominent media presence in the Canal Zone.[10]

Baxter's self-description plus the self-referential name *Macwalbax*, drawn from the first syllable of each of the three contributors' surnames, casts a vision of a group of white men comfortable in their role as influencers and proud of their commitment to speaking the truths others might think to silence out of culturally enforced politeness. As authors, editors, publishers, and at least one Ivy League graduate, it is safe to say that these men did not feel any need for shame or embarrassment regarding their personal opinions on life in the Canal Zone. Today *Macwalbax* survives in a few archives and, tellingly, the humor collection of the San Francisco Public Library. There is no significant analysis of its contents to date. It is built of the doggerel poetry of John McGroarty, cartoons by M. H. Walsh, and selected "Commentary Pro and Con, Mostly Con" by Baxter. Theirs was not the only work combining cartoonish depictions of canal life with accompanying doggerel poetry published by the Panama Times. Sue Core and Ann Cordts McKeown gathered their "sketches and accompanying jingles" originally distributed as part of the "Isthmiana by Susanna" feature of *The Panama American* in the book *Isthmiana* in 1939.[11] Core was also known for her memoir collection of similar work, *Maid in Panama*, published by Claremont Press in the United States in 1938. Such frequency of publication shows a clear desire on the part of readers for this style of anecdotes and reflections on life at the canal. The late fifteenth-century Portuguese portrayal of Black bodies as dogs lends a particularly painful irony to the encapsulation of West Indian women in doggerel poetry (see chapter 2). Even puns have the capacity for diminishment.

Rounsevell was aware of the West Indian community as part of the complex interwoven needs that might be served by a publishing company at the time. His depiction of the population is unsurprising: a type of sanitized paternalism that unflinchingly holds fast to a vision of the West Indian community as inherently enslaved. From the unearned privilege of his social location, he also believed that the West Indian residents of the Canal Zone had little contact with Americans in their day-to-day living.[12] One assumes that Black women working as domestics, hotel managers, cooks, laundresses, and sex workers would disagree. While describing the many facets of society impacting his work in the Canal Zone, Rounsevell writes,

> Last, but not least, in numerical importance is a populous group of foreign Negroes, brought from the British and French West Indies as laborers in the construction and operation of the Panama Railroad and the Panama Canal. Meek, hard-working plodders, underpaid free slaves in an environment the making of which goes back for centuries, they are practically indispensable in the operation of the Canal and in all other enterprises or industries requiring great volumes of common labor.[13]

Rounsevell may have considered his position progressive at the time, yet it still bears dehumanizing tropes that portray a lack of agency, resignation to circumstance, and perfunctory absolution of his own self-responsibility for benefiting from a system that "goes back for centuries." The language of "hard-working plodders" utilizes the same agency-reducing imagery generally reserved for farm animals laboring to plow a field for human benefit.

Rounsevell's perspectives are echoed in the works published by the Panama Times. Those stereotypical depictions and commentaries on a variety of lived experiences in the Canal Zone, including the common Eurocentric

devaluation of West Indian life, unsurprisingly contain strong environmental/
natural themes in their representation of West Indian women. Scholars have
well documented the dehumanization of Black women through their connection to Earth (see chapter 2) and here we see it played out in the specific
displacement of West Indian women to the Panamá Canal through the stereotyping of their creativity and wisdom in the ways that they "made do" in
those times.

Macwalbax, specifically, is a 128-page collection covering a range of top-
ics and perspectives, only a fraction of which acknowledge the myriad ways
that West Indian labor upheld American lifestyles. In fairness, there is a
satirical tone to the entire work, not solely in those pages stereotyping Black
bodies and livelihoods, and the authors went as far as portraying themselves
in cartoon form and in text at the start of the collection.[14] Overall the tenor of
the book is one that claims significant authority, where even in the predictable
meter of doggerel poetry the opinions of the writers are put forth as significant and influential, with a higher value placed on their own understanding of
truth than on conventional niceties that might otherwise be expected in a less
controversial form. *Macwalbax* is meant to be titillating and a bit risqué. The
white men contributing to this volume of stereotyping snapshots cannot seem
to help but style themselves as superior to all that they observe. The visage of
the West Indian woman is thrown into this toxic white masculinity and left
vulnerable to uninformed interpretation. And yet here still we can find echoes
of her real value that illustrate an important baseline for other expressions in
the historical record.

Members of the West Indian community, counter to their own self-
understanding, are routinely portrayed in *Macwalbax* as simpleminded,
slightly devious, and primarily defined by their labor. Because the work most
visible to Americans in the Canal Zone was centered on the vending, cooking, and provision of food, and the laundering of clothes in natural waters,
many portrayals of West Indian women routinely connected their existence
with the conspicuous presence of the land itself.[15] There was a range of
entrepreneurial labor undertaken by West Indian women at the time, and
many worked in domestic service and for hotels, as can be seen in the 1906
affidavits of migrant women from Martinique (see chapter 2). Olive Senior
notes that increased literacy rates among Jamaican women by the close of
the nineteenth century meant that clerical roles such as "teachers, midwives,
hoteliers, businesswomen, secretaries, and clerks" likely also were repre-
sented among women migrating to work at the canal. While service roles
predominate in the historical record, administrative labor also was central to
the work of the community.[16] Yet the conflation of Black women's bodies
with Earth, and through that connection with nurturance and ease, remained
an essentializing norm in the portrayal of West Indian women.

This central trope of the white imaginary is captured in images across the Caribbean at the time of canal construction, with West Indian women cast as nearly inseparable from Earth. The agential figure of the "black market woman" is used by art historian and African American studies scholar Krista Thompson in her exploration of popular tropical tropes constructed to invite tourists' gaze.[17] In her work on the intentional tropicalization of Jamaica and the Bahamas, Thompson unpacks the American imaginary and its transformation of the "picturesque" in art and photography throughout the British colonial era as well as its impact on postcolonial imagery. She identifies the "black market woman" as a primary visual representation of tropical nature in the Bahamas during this time. Thompson pairs this trope with photographs and paintings from the early twentieth century, often depicting Black women stylistically arranged with familiar representations of the tropical wilderness—palm fronds, flowers, and ocean waves. The ubiquitous basket is seen carried on women's heads or in their hands, containing chickens, flowers, and fruit for white consumption. These "currencies of paradise" are clearly portrayed in an iconic photograph by Jacob Frank Coonley, "On the Way to Market."[18] The construction of the "black market woman" becomes the very definition of a tropical paradise—one where the waters are inviting, the food is plentiful, and every exoticized thing is an offering for tourists' pleasure.

As Thompson insists, "The black market woman and nature are connected, if not equated . . . [and] the visual equation of the black market woman figure is even more explicit in paintings of the island."[19] Thompson further traces the erasure of the Black woman as a figure distinct from nature over time in the work of US artist Winslow Homer in the late 1800s. Homer begins with classic black market women figures centered in his work, but over time portrays them in an impressionistic manner such that they "become parts of the representation of nature."[20] This action renders Black women no longer central or primary, but simply one more lush offering in the tropical picturesque. The visual equation of Black women with nature built successfully upon written travel accounts that sexualized the tropics through association with the Black woman's body and sexual intercourse.[21] The implications of such coconstructions of race, class, gender, and the natural world (what I have named ecocreolization) followed women from the Bahamas and Jamaica to Panamá in the early 1900s as they crossed the waters seeking work at the canal. Thompson confronts the erasure of Black women's bodies (as just one example among many challenging aspects of tropicalization and the Caribbean picturesque) as a way to interrogate the interwoven evolutions of art, tourism, and the American imaginary. Her example of the black market woman offers ecowomanism a powerful analytical tool to rehumanize community, reclaim valuation, and further the argument for inherited environmental cultures in the work of environmental ethics.[22]

By the time of *Macwalbax*'s publication, such imaginaries were firmly rooted in the minds of white Americans, and while much of the art in *Macwalbax* is intentionally cartoonish, the tropes remain familiar. Even in the offerings where West Indian women were not central, cast simply as one aspect of the day-to-day lived experience of the contributors, their depictions in word and art echo a reduction to the utility of their labor and association with the land. In "Carnival Days in Panama" (see appendix B), the scene is set to include the range of people who allow themselves to let go of care and worry in the final days before Lent. Here, "high and low and rich and poor / In festive mood unite" and "denizens of every race" are described as "proud to claim a pompous place / In the Carnival parade."[23] Yet the washerwoman's description, intended to represent a West Indian woman as seen in "The Wash Lady," is still reduced to a simple acceptance of her assigned task. Even during carnival season, when categories and norms are supposedly sidelined in favor of celebration, "the humble washerwoman / In her simple honest heart / Is happily convinced that she / Performs a vital part." All other characters, from the "common laborer" to the "ancient dame," the "matron," and even the "lovely Aida / For the nonce, our royal Queen," are elevated for a time in communal festivity.[24] But here the washerwoman remains intentionally cast out, deluded in her supposed simplicity that hers is a vital role. There is no art accompanying this piece of doggerel poetry in the text.

The labor of food provision also continues to hold true to stereotyped form in "Panama's Market Place" (see appendix B), where descriptions of a range of racialized vendors collect to describe a bustling market. This poem, in its final stanza, concludes:

So wags the weary world along, so grind the ruthless mills
Of Fate that knows not sympathy, with human hopes nor ills;
In Panama's old market place where crude and vivid souls
Depict the Human Comedy in all it's [*sic*] varied roles.[25]

The roles are meant to be definitive, and to define a series of norms in a community made up of an unusual mix of peoples and cultures due to the historic complexity of labor requirements at the site of the largest investment of capital in any project outside of war in human history. In this piece, the West Indian woman is defined in a full stanza as an innate keeper of the home and all things domestic. Yet something of her unassailable dignity still shines through the rhyming couplets.

The negro woman, Junoesque, proceeds with stately tread,
A basket full of merchandise upon her kinky head;

Her generous rotundity fills up the narrow aisle,
Disarming all resentment by her broad and potent smile.[26]

The trope of West Indian women painted as round, smiling domestics whose ceaseless performative kindness somehow saves them from the resentment that should logically be their due continues here, even with the overtone of majestic movement and outward friendliness utilized by the poet. Couching such essentialized roles in the language of Roman divinity, "Junoesque," does not lessen the odiousness of both the devaluation of domestic work and the assumption that appeasement is logically necessary to make the West Indian woman's body and labor palatable to others in the marketplace. While Juno lends an aura of divinity, she also extends an association with inherent housekeeping duties and domestic work. No amount of stately movement, for all that we are likely meant to find irony in such grace, erases the primary markers of textured hair and lushly curved embodiment that center this depiction. West Indian women are characterized, once again, as naturally displaced in place (see chapter 1) by their bodies, their roles, and the expectation that they appease those around them for daring to take up space.

The Black body is displaced in place through its equation with nonhuman nature and comparison to norms of hegemonic whiteness that presume white superiority. The first offering in *Macwalbax* centered entirely on the West Indian woman as a caricature is "The Wash Lady," aforementioned (see appendix B). Its opening stanza builds an image of the West Indian woman through negation, drawing on the name "Daisy" as a double entendre to depict how she is *not* white (like a Daisy's petals), *not* blonde (like the yellow carpels of a Daisy), and most certainly *not* expected to claim a defining role in society.

No Nordic blonde, with bright blue eyes,
That hold the tints of summer skies,
And golden hair and dainty size,
      Is Daisy;
My heroine is not that kind;
On sentimental stuff, I find,
Her practical, prosaic mind
      Is hazy[27];

While flowers often represent an insufficiently nuanced expression of femininity, it is important to note that Daisy continues to be defined through Earth-centered images, even if flowers at first pass seem less dehumanizing

than laboring farm animals or dogs (see chapter 2). Daisies are unsophisti-
cated in the human valuation of flowers, and our Daisy does not even measure
up to a flower often reserved for young girls. This narrative contains other
traditionally dismissive tropes where the reader is expected to embrace the
familiar deprecation of Black women as physically imperfect (via the hegemonic norms of white skin, blonde hair, blue eyes, and petite body shape)
with uncultured minds.[28] The writer is so taken with his pun that he continues
to pontificate on how the subject of the poem might have been given a host
of other names, but alas,

in her frail and helpless youth,
Some joker, with a taste uncouth,
Must dub her "Daisy," though, in truth,
            She's rather shady.[29]

His wordplay, which once again highlights the wash lady's skin as too dark
to warrant the name of a bright, white flower, also insists on linking that rich-
ness of hue with underhandedness.

"Shady" is a noteworthy choice of adjective to describe Daisy's melanated
skin, and its double meaning guides the reader through a carefree devaluation
of Daisy's labor through the rest of the poem. First, her work is described
as both simplistic and destructive. After insisting that her "strenuous" and
"dusky" body would naturally reject the use of a washing machine (presum-
ably because Daisy's practical and foggy mind is incapable of understanding
the utility of such a tool), the author devalues her hardiness.

She has the strength to tear and rend
My wardrobe, scant, from end to end,
But small indeed, her power to mend—
            She seldom sews.[30]

The text casts the wash lady as less advanced in her labors, with uncivilized
accusations reminiscent of predatory anthropological descriptions of less
technologically advanced cultures. "Her apparatus is but rude; / Her working
methods, quaintly crude."[31] Finally, the writer despairs how Daisy leaves his
clothes to dry outdoors, laid flat on the vegetation. He captures her lack of
concern with his comfort ("And that's why cockle burs and seeds / Adorn my
B.V.D's") in doggerel stanzas, yet finishes by admitting to his own failure in
that "finding fault is vain."[32] We are meant to celebrate the writer's civility
through his magnanimous expression of love for Daisy that completes the text
even while cataloging Daisy's faults to the very end. The wash lady is characterized as a tool herself, one that fades into the landscape of the everyday

and cannot even understand the utility of a machine that would replace her labor. Like the rest of creation, she is understood to be present for the comfort and service of white men without a single "soulful yearning" to lead her to a more fulfilling life.[33]

This dismissive description of the wash lady spares not a single word to describe the immense toil, risk, and disregard faced by those who worked cleaning laundry in the Canal Zone. Historian Eyra Marcela Reyes Rivas describes the work of laundresses as underpaid, physically challenging, undertaken in unsanitary conditions, and as labor that exposed workers to both racial and social discrimination.[34] It also provided an avenue for their minimization and erasure. Historian Joan Flores-Villalobos notes that the archival record is replete with postcards capturing life during canal construction through photography. As with much of the historical record, West Indian women were rarely the focus of such depictions, yet were often included in the background as part of the scenery. In her description of a postcard of the Canal Commission's sanitarium on Taboga Island, Flores-Villalobos notes the inclusion of West Indian women almost as an afterthought:

The women at the laundry seem to exist in a 'jungle' beyond the civilizing force of the canal commission . . . as if to reiterate that West Indian women's bodies in the zone were naturally available as the objects of gendered racial difference to American Viewers.[35]

As an invitation to the white gaze that reduced their bodies to the same land Americans were seeking to "tame" in the name of civilization, depictions of West Indian laundry workers served to further undermine their full humanity and voice.

The visual that accompanies "The Wash Lady" (see appendix B) furthers the stereotype of simplistic reduction to labor for the ease and comfort of others. Here Daisy is drawn in the foreground of the image, with stereotypical cultural markers and a stylized form that signals Blackness through dark skin, thick lips, the use of a kerchief, and an ample body type. The load of laundry on Daisy's head is larger than her entire body, and her focus remains on the reader. Behind Daisy are reminders of everyday life, but her gaze is turned away from them all. Neither the stereotypically drawn West Indian man behind her nor the donkey at its labors pulling a cart nor the work building, house, tree, or land in the background capture Daisy's mind. Her only care is balancing the laundry on her head and the attention of those reading about the irony of her name. She is not drawn as part of the landscape in the ways accomplished by the black market woman trope described above, yet neither does she share space with white Americans in this image. Neither the laundry on her head nor the river where she labors are part of the supposedly civilized lived experience of the writer. The wash lady must experience the most intimate parts of his clothing (the tactlessly mentioned BVDs) yet finds herself valued solely through the performance of the author's own morality as he casts off the vanity of "finding fault" to ironically close his piece with the proclamation, "With all your faults, / I love you still, / Oh Daisy dear."[36] This measure of love falls woefully short of regard that accounts for the full dignity and humanity of Daisy.

Macwalbax embraces the black market woman picturesque in the very next offering, which is also the only other poem in the book that is fully dedicated to a West Indian woman. "The Banana Lady" harkens back to the artistic tropes of the black market woman through its visual representation of a food vendor. In the accompanying illustration (see appendix B), the rendering of the woman's facial features is much more realistic, and less cartoonish, than that drawn for "The Wash Lady." The banana lady's facial features would be plausibly recognizable to someone who knows her. She too is round yet strong, but in a way reminiscent of an actual human body. Her hair is tied, as was often traditional, and she is depicted as seated behind her wares. The banana lady, literally named for a part of nonhuman nature, serves as the background of her own illustration. The mangos and bananas before her are the highlights of the image. Like Coonley's photograph and Homer's water-color, this line drawing emphasizes Thompson's "currencies of paradise" expected by the tourist's, or ex-patriot's, gaze.

The poem opens with a confirmation of Thompson's argument.
Oh you quaint Banana Lady, with the turban and the smile,
    And the tray of toothsome merchandise, in appetizing pile,
First glimpse of "local color," for the tourist's eager gaze,
    And picturesque example of the lure of tropic ways.[37]

This unnamed food vendor becomes the center of a complicated two steps that define her in relation to nonhuman nature but ensures that she is valued lower than the plant life she sells. Her self-determination and indisputable dignity also have a role in this depiction, yet the author is careful to equate the most venerated black-skinned women of his own imagination with the same underhandedness and simplistic acceptance alleged of West Indian women earlier in the book. The author waxes poetic about the fruits in the foreground of the piece, then delights in the further devaluation of the banana lady herself. "Oh the succulent banana is a delicacy rare / And the fresh and fragrant mango is a treat beyond compare" to the travelers in various military and tourist roles arriving in Panamá.[38] Of the banana lady he then writes,

Your homely, pleasant features are a vision of delight;
    Your patient, pensive attitude is restful to the sight;

Your black and beaming countenance, impassive and serene,
>   Would grace a Moorish Princess, or an Abyssinian Queen.[39]

One would prefer she'd made a scene.

    Yet this West Indian woman appears unconcerned with the author's gaze. Her eyes are looking to the left, away from those who would consume her image for their own tropical fantasies. Perhaps that is why the author goes to such lengths in his failed attempt to undermine the dignity and strength not only of this one vendor but of the little he knows of her inherited cultures.

Famed Cleopatra, in her barge, upon the classic Nile,
>   Had no more regal stateliness, no more bewitching guile,
Than you can defly [*sic*] bring to bear, when, artfully betimes,
>   You separate the public from their nickles [*sic*] and their dimes.

But, in your idle moments, whence that dignity, profound,
>   So mystic and inscrutable, that girds you round and round?
Do you perhaps inherit that inimitable poise
>   From some dead Nubian chieftain, past human griefs and joys?[40]

Something of the transgenerational survival and strength born of the wisdom of our mothers' mothers, more than historic royalty or political leaders, both stymies and intrigues the writer. He returns to tired tropes of the tragic Black woman who is at the same time happy with her lot in life to describe the banana lady's inner resilience.

Behind those somber, brooding eyes, that dark and stolid face,
>   Persists the ancient tragedy and sorrow of your race;
But in your wise philosophy, there dwells no vengeful hate,
>   As you sell your ripe bananas, smilling [*sic*] cheerily at Fate.
Oh for the calm serenity that marks thy simple soul;
>   Oh for thy heart, contented, that accepts a humble role;
Oh for thy cheerful spirit that makes any life worth while;
>   Oh thou quaint Banana Lady, with the turban and the smile.[41]

The author clearly longs for the same wisdom of knowing.

    Between these stanzas, an ecowomanist analysis of Latina and Black women's own inherited cultural wisdom offers profound resources embedded in our communal histories and stories to defy the dehumanizing forces of enslavement, colonization, and neo-imperialism. Beyond the defamatory insinuation that it is duplicity and a lack of mental capacity—rather than dignity and strength—that create such an ability to survive the incomprehensible in this market vendor lies a wealth of values to bring to bear in a time of climate disruption. These values must be rescued from the dismissive generations of white Americans who could not understand the wealth carried within Black bodies. Instead we are called, ancestrally, to embrace moving through life with a serenity that undermines both apathy to environmental devastation and faith in last-minute technological interventions to the exclusion of efforts requiring sacrifice in our lifestyles. We too must find a way to accept a humble role, not because of violence and racialization but because of our coconstruction and relation to Earth. Survival must supplant vengeance.

Macwalbax was never intended to serve as a defining commentary on the lives of West Indian women at the site of the canal. Its engagement with their lived experiences is as cursory as the relationships its authors built across racial lines. Yet the opinions of these three men influenced white Americans with every weekly serial. Their words served to undermine both West Indian women and Earth, among others, through a use of humor and supposed cleverness that easily spreads through human communities as entertainment. These are the cultural tools that sharpen and maintain hegemonies in times of change. At their most insidious, these are also the implements of justification for easy comfort with the status quo. An ecowomanist ethic bears the pain of wrestling with such immense transgenerational violence in order to replant the seeds of transgenerational wisdom that are too strong to fully erase. Where white men violated both West Indian women and Earth through self-righteousness, dehumanization, greed, and profound disregard, white women did so just as ruthlessly as part of their own struggle to survive the unimaginable. Their failure to center that which keeps us all whole serves as a reminder to elevate values promoting communal resilience and survival in Latina and Black women's histories. Due to hegemonic norms, white women's stories survive in the archives, woven together with their interpretations of silenced histories.

PANAMA CANAL BRIDE AND THE ENDARKENMENT OF THE WHITE WOMAN'S GAZE

The construction of the Panamá Canal recommenced under US leadership at a time when Americans avidly consumed travel memoirs, relying on the subjective experiences of writers for entertainment and insight into the unknown.[42] For white women with enough socioeconomic privilege to travel by choice, writing offered the opportunity to reflect on various interconnected aspects of identity in their daily living. While their accounts necessarily center on the cultural expectations dictated by gender, class, and race at the time of their travels, they also offer echoes of identity and self-understanding among the individuals encountered on their journeys.[43] Such expectations, whether expressed as the presumed cultural superiority of the writer or the otherized difference of everyone else, are conveyed through embodiment and the need to maintain separation between the writers' bodies and everything they experience as foreign.[44] I argue that travel memoirs simultaneously demonstrate the impact of land on the authors themselves and those they encounter along the way. Earth itself plays a central role in the unfolding of women's travel memoirs. Earth becomes a central figure by offering challenges and opportunities for self-awareness that would not exist in stories solely emphasizing human engagement. Travel writing differs from diaspora and migration literatures, yet relates in terms of structure. While it brings the complexities of privilege and assumed superiorities into written form, such biases are not only visible to the reader but capture intersectional oppressions through the traveler's gaze.[45] The voluntary nature of travel aids our understanding of the interrelated constructions of gender, race, class, and environmental culture by sidelining complexities that necessarily arise in the face of forced migration.

Elizabeth Kittredge Parker offers a travel memoir of her time as a newlywed in Panamá during the early years of canal construction under US leadership. The struggles to build the canal strongly influence her work, yet she intentionally focuses on the daily lives surrounding those efforts. Parker leaves the analysis of the engineering to those doing that work. Her writings instead illustrate household maintenance, the transplantation of US cultural norms and lifestyles to Panamá, and the development of community adjacent to the canal. As with other white women writing at the time, Parker unintentionally captures wisdom and survival skills among West Indian women working as domestics in the early 1900s. Olive Senior notes the particular importance of these working relationships for understanding West Indian women's lives at the canal: "It was in the domestic environment that the clash of cultures, of color, of class, probably became the most pronounced."[46] These meeting points in day-to-day living demonstrate the interwoven development of race, gender, class, and environmental culture through the stereotypes projected by white women employers and the resistance, dignity, and self-awareness of the West Indian women working as domestics. As with many other white writers of the era, Parker refers to the West Indian and Indigenous Panamanian women she encounters in Panamá solely by their first names. Therefore, in the pages that follow I will refer to all of the characters in Parker's story, including Parker herself, by first name.

Panama Canal Bride: A Story of Construction Days was published almost thirty years later than *Macwalbax*, but Elizabeth's memoir begins in February 1907 with her first impressions of Panamá.[47] On arrival, she notes the "palm trees, red-tiled roofs, and the blue, blue Caribbean that surrounds the boat."[48] Her arrival is a relief to her after two years of separation from her fiancé, Charlie, who delayed her migration to Panamá in the wake of multiple epidemics that had befallen and even killed other canal officials' wives.[49] It is immediately clear that Elizabeth carries with her the hegemonic norms of white America. Rather than describing herself as an unusual arrival in a tropical land, she recounts the phenotypes of those around her as alien. While on a train away from the boat that brought her to Panamá she remembers, "I caught fleeting glimpses of alien faces—slanting eyes, brown-skinned Aryan features, smiling black kinky-haired people."[50] While those same faces are also those of outsiders to Panamá, brought to the land to work on the canal, it is their divergence from the assumed norms of her own whiteness that captures Elizabeth's attention. She marries Charlie the following day.[51]

Panama Canal Bride tells us little about Elizabeth's life in New England before her arrival at the canal—not even her name before marriage—yet she characterizes her impressions of Panamá primarily by differences from the expectations of her former life. Charlie's friends arrive by train for their wedding, a simple affair conducted in the home of a coworker.[52] During the festivities following the ceremony, Elizabeth has her first encounter with a West Indian woman in domestic service.

> As we sat down to our wedding breakfast, I was aware of more contrasts—the long table on the narrow screened porch, thick white china, plated silver, *pâté de fois gras,* champagne, roast turkey—all served awkwardly by a little Jamaican maid in a gingham dress.[53]

The canal itself immediately becomes a primary character in her story. Everyone in attendance at her wedding is present in Panamá because of the canal, focuses their thinking and conversation on the canal's problems and progress, and lives their lives with the canal as their primary priority.[54] This human-driven rupture of Earth's natural state gains the weight of personality in her recollections.

On the first morning of her married life Elizabeth meets Sarah, the Jamaican maid her husband had hired to assist them in the home. Elizabeth remembers that

> a youthful black girl was standing in the kitchen doorway, her kinky hair neatly braided in tiny pigtails all over her head. Her stiffly starched cotten [*sic*] dress was partly covered with a clean white apron, the corner of which she was nervously twisting in her strong black hands.[55]

Sarah has reason to be nervous. Even though a woman named Lizzie who worked as a domestic in the house of one of Charlie's colleagues had trained her, Elizabeth has complete control over her employment.[56] As a recent arrival, Elizabeth does not understand the work of maintaining a household in the Canal Zone. She has a hard time understanding Sarah's speech and is surprised by the "ugly black iron stove" that requires coal and kindling to function.[57] The processes of ordering coal and kindling, food from the supply ships traveling back and forth to New York, and local foodstuffs from roaming vendors are all new experiences for Elizabeth.[58]

The Panamá Canal brides (white women who moved to Panamá to support their husbands' work on the canal) that Elizabeth meets assume a clear superiority of knowledge and lifestyle over the West Indian women in their employ. Elizabeth soon learns from fellow canal bride Kay Jackson that her own inability to understand Sarah is not uncommon. Kay also disparages the survival knowledge of the women working on her behalf.

> "I can't understand Jamaican. Can you? It's not only the *h*'s in the wrong places, it's the inflection also."
>
> "No," said Kay. "I've been here six months and I still can't understand what my maid, Jane, wants when I go to the commissary. I've had two girls already," she continued. "They seem so stupid, but when I tried to do without one, I decided they weren't so dumb after all. We have to realize they've never seen the inside of a civilized home before. They've always cooked on charcoal braziers, washed their clothes in the river, and used gourds for dishes."[59]

From an outside, ahistorical lens, it seems absurd that women uprooted from their own environmental knowledge would mock the skills of those working in an area much closer to their own lived experience. The racist imaginary that black-skinned women are somehow inherently suited to hard labor in the tropics does not translate here to an assumed ability to acquire, prepare, and serve food in a tropical region barely domesticated to a white American lifestyle. This encounter takes place only two years past the time when Elizabeth's husband had refused to bring her to Panamá because of high fatality rates from mosquito-borne diseases. The Isthmian Canal Commission is working hard to "tame" nature to meet American standards of civilization yet still Elizabeth describes her home and community in terms of hardship, lack of resources, and struggle. Her personal opinions are regularly expressed in cheerful, excited tones yet she places the language of maladaptation in the mouths of most other white characters in her book. Still, her instincts, along with those of other white women in similar circumstances, assume the innate superiority of her own way of life. Such assumptions continue to undermine environmental efforts in the present day when an inability to sustain a shift in lifestyle, often due to the expectations of cultural hegemonic norms, subverts the intentions of those who genuinely seek a balanced relationship with Earth. Ecowomanist ethics centers the inherited environmental cultures of those regularly pushed to the margins as a corrective to cataclysmic narratives of white superiority.

Delusions of white superiority characterize what Elizabeth names "the Battle of the Insects" throughout her text. Here again the impact of mosquitos is central to canal life, and she celebrates the saga of their control as the conquest and civilizing success of the Panamá Canal Zone Sanitation Commission. But mosquitos are not the only small denizens of Earth impacting US attempts to dominate the land. Elizabeth also describes her struggles with fleas and roaches, and how ants thwart her early attempts at gardening:

> With New England zeal, I decided to grow some vegetables. I planted the seeds and was delighted to see the little plants growing so fast. But, alas, one morning, I found nothing but stems. Every single green leaf had disappeared during the night. I noticed a tiny narrow path from my garden to a climb of nearby bushes. Scurrying back and forth were black ants; each one leaving the garden was covered with a piece of green leaf.[60]

Elizabeth then encounters a Chinese food vendor who commiserates with her about the ants. Instead of attempting to learn from his labors, his statement that he works continually to keep them out of his garden is enough to justify her retreat from relationship with Earth. "I decided the umbrella ants were too much of a problem for me and I gave up trying to raise any vegetables."[61] The failures of her own experience and knowing regularly cause Elizabeth to pay others for services that she devalues rather than learn new skills to fit the situation.

Even as Sarah demonstrates the ability to do several tasks competently through methods well suited to the Panamá Canal environment, Elizabeth remains focused on Sarah's failures. Almost all of Sarah's errors are connected to class markers transported to Panamá from outside the country: "She insisted on using my best Irish linen napkins for scrub cloths. She cleaned my new silver with Sapolio. She melted the bottom off my silver coffee pot, a wedding gift, by putting it on the stove to dry."[62] The day that Sarah's inability to read causes her to cook fish for a dinner party using floor oil rather than cooking oil (the two bottles were identical save for their labels) is the last day that she serves in Elizabeth's employ.[63] Sarah's illiteracy surprises Elizabeth, who replaces her with a sixteen-year-old Indigenous girl named Mercedes. Mercedes lasts only two days, leaving Elizabeth to tend the house alone for the first time.[64]

Elizabeth's attempts at simple food preparation result in a string of failures and embarrassment that serve as a key moment of transition during her time in Panamá. She describes most of the experience in terms of *blackness* and *shame*. Everything becomes dirty and black in the face of this struggle, including Elizabeth herself. On the morning following Mercedes's departure, Elizabeth awakens to the realization that she will have to attend to the tasks of the day alone. She has to "tackle the ugly black stove and the dirty soft coal."[65] Elizabeth has a master's degree in astronomy but has never built a fire. She fleetingly hopes that Charlie will attend to the stove, but soon understands that domestic duties are part of his expectations of her as his wife. In the face of the actual experience, it is Sarah's wisdom that best applies. Predictably, Elizabeth once again fails to value what Sarah already knows.

> I went out "ter marsh hup de coal." I had never built a fire before but I had a vague idea that if I could get the kindling started, all would be well. Alas, when I dumped a shovelful of coal on, the black powder smothered the blaze, as Sarah had warned.[66]

Elizabeth finally succeeds with a bit of practice only to encounter Charlie who immediately laughs at her, sending her to the bathroom mirror. "I gazed at the black smudges on my forehead and cheeks, where little trickles of perspiration had left little irregular streaks of white. I joined in Charlie's laughter but, at the moment, it didn't seem awfully funny."[67] Elizabeth finds herself literally blackened by the work of preparing a simple meal. This unintended blackface causes her shame, and her response is to remind herself that she is a housewife with a "trained mind," who is "supposed to be able to solve mundane problems."[68] Her determination leads her to practice until she gains the ability to maintain a coal fire throughout the day. It is lived experience and not her academic training or cultural standards that leads, finally, to success.

After Mercedes comes just one more Indigenous Panamanian woman, Rafaela, but she also does not stay long. Following Rafaela's departure Elizabeth and Charlie contract with West Indian men to support the upkeep of the house, and Elizabeth's reflections on West Indian women's labors almost completely cease in the text.[69] The one exception is Mimi, the family's nanny, who makes an appearance nearly five years later when the canal is almost complete and the Parkers have had three children. Faced with a mudslide between her location and the Parkers' new home, Mimi refuses to cross the mud. "No, suh, . . . I doan' go. . . I'se goin' back ter Jamaica, suh," is all Elizabeth bothers to record of Mimi's experience.[70] Mimi finally relents for a promised measure of brandy when she reaches the new house.[71] It is noteworthy that with time Elizabeth recognizes the prejudice that drives her engagement with those she considers other to her own knowing. Once she feels her home life is stable, she realizes, "I was beginning to understand the natives better and to have more sympathy for their points of view. They became human beings to me—no longer the strange unfathomable creatures they had at first seemed."[72] We have no way of knowing if this rehumanizing perspective extended to the West Indian community as well. Likely not, given the lack of similar commentary in the text. The diversity of communities racialized as Black at the site of the canal draws from centuries of history that still impact Black Panamanians to this day. West Indian migrants in search of work were long held as outsiders even by the descendants of Spanish enslavement who remained in Panamá. The reality of being eternally displaced in place significantly impacts the West Indian community's evolving self-understanding (see "Reaping the Sweets").

The remainder of *Panama Canal Bride* focuses on the unrelenting journey of canal construction itself. Elizabeth's memoir ends with a boat ride among the privileged few who are taken for a test run of the canal twelve days before its official launch. At the successful completion of the boat's journey, Elizabeth celebrates that a "dream of centuries had come true."[73] She is proud of the engineering achievements required to successfully construct the canal and gratified by the technological advances that have "civilized" the land to a standard of American living she now recognizes. The closer Panamá comes to the norms of her former life in Boston, the less she troubles herself to comment on the West Indian women whose labors make her lifestyle possible. The knowledge production of generations of women learning to survive by learning the land and its realities across various forms of forced displacement fades into the background of a society built on the drowned corpse of the jungle. It is unreasonable to argue that a white woman's memoir offers a full perspective into the lived experiences, inherited wisdom, and knowledge production of West Indian women working at the site of the canal. Nevertheless, such recollections offer important insights into what West Indian women suffered at the hands of their employers while working to support themselves. Such messages are internalized over time and impact the construction of identity across the intersectional influences of gender, race, and the environment.

"Reaping the Sweets": Inherited Environmental Culture in Their Own Words

> I remember so many things but all I have to do now is give God thanks and praise because I can see that He has been with us, with the West Indians, all along the way. And He has brought them now . . . many of them they have their offspring here now, that are reaping the sweets.[74]

In 2018, Barbadian filmmaker Alison Saunders released a documentary seeking to reclaim the stories of Barbadians who migrated to Panamá to work on the canal. *Panama Dreams* centers on the story of Saunders's own family member Prince Collymore, who left Barbados in 1907 to find work in Panamá. Saunders tells Collymore's story as a way to gain insight into important ancestral legacies that are missing from the historical record.[75] She describes the migration of over 150,000 West Indians from across the Caribbean to Panamá as one of the most impactful events in Caribbean history. Saunders believes that too many are no longer connected to those who departed for the isthmus, and we who remain have much to learn from the dreams and drive of those who labored on the canal. She began her research for the documentary in June 2011, following a trip to Cuba that highlighted for her just how many people from across the Caribbean have ancestral ties to Panamá.[76] Her integrity in her research and her belief in the intellectual property rights of the family are how I am blessed to have unpublished video footage of Ronica Campbell, Kady Grant, and Irie Davis—all pseudonyms for members of my own extended family—speaking about their experiences as young women whose parents worked on the canal. Ronica Campbell was ninety-two at the time of her interview.[77] Saunders gave my family an incomparable gift when she shared video footage of their conversation. The reclamation of such priceless legacies is part of the dream behind Saunders's work, and we are grateful.

Ronica Campbell, Irie Davis, and Kady Grant were sisters whose parents migrated from Barbados in 1908 or 1909 to work on the Panamá Canal.[78] Their father, Eldon Miller, worked on the canal and married Chandice Rowe Miller (both also pseudonyms) when she arrived from Barbados.[79] Chandice Rowe Miller worked doing laundry for Americans who were laboring on the canal.[80] Once Eldon Miller married and left the bachelors' housing facilities, the family established itself in the Low Quarters of Gatún. They lived right beside the canal, near the Gatún Locks, and all three sisters acknowledge that life was often hard. The Millers had six children, and Eldon Miller experienced the injustice that so many West Indians faced during canal construction of unequal pay and unequal access to higher-level positions.[81] The infamous silver roll listed employees of the canal who in theory were not US citizens, the argument being that those on the gold roll needed vacation time in the United States to recuperate each year. But the silver and gold rolls soon divided along racial lines regardless of citizenship, echoing racial segregation back in the United States.[82] In the words of Ronica Campbell, "The Americans got higher pay, and they were usually the higher ones, the bosses and so of the West Indians."[83] The salary was too low to support a family with six children, and the sisters know it was the Millers' ingenuity that kept the family fed, housed, and grateful for what they had.

Relationship with Earth plays a central role in the recollected story of the Millers' life on the canal. They lived in shared housing, in buildings that sheltered four families at once with bathrooms and other amenities outside of the main structure. The sisters' facial expressions show some lingering embarrassment about the living conditions of the time and also great pride in the resilience and success of their family in the face of imposed hardships. At one point, Ronica Campbell acknowledges that she does not like to speak about such things, even with her own children. It is hard to tell whether she means discussing bathrooms, living where the roads were still mud paths, or sharing space with other families. There is collective laughter at the mention of eating codfish—at nine cents a pound, it was the food that the family could afford. With some prompting from Saunders, it soon becomes clear that the source of the sisters' survival, well-being, and sense of inherited pride is directly tied to their father's skill and dedication at farming and their mother's ability to create food for the family even when resources were scarce.[84]

Survival in relationship to land serves as a foundation of inherited environmental cultures in this family history. Preparing their food directly from Earth while laboring under the intense conditions of canal construction provides a foundation of great pride. As Irie Davis put it,

> What I always say—the Barbadians are ingenious people. I learned that from my parents. They are ingenious. They knew how to live because if they didn't know how to live, a lot of us would have been dead. A lot of the children. But they knew how to live.[85]

Eldon Miller lived by working on his farm every day, as Irie Davis described:

> My father was such an ingenious man. . . . He had a big farm and he farmed all kinds of vegetables and root food. And we didn't go hungry because of that. You see? He made sure. And he went to his farm every day in his life. He went to that farm. Sometimes he worked in the mornings on the Panamá Canal and in the afternoons and evenings he went to his farm and worked. When he worked nights on the Panamá Canal, he went to his farm in the mornings and worked. And he always brought food home for us. So we were never hungry.[86]

The Millers grew plantains, yams, and bananas. Ronica Campbell's expression shows real delight as she remembers her father's yams. "I always tell my children about the yams . . . he had some yams that I never see again, some large yams he would bring home."[87] On days when there was little else to eat, Chandice Rowe Miller would climb breadfruit trees planted by the Americans around the living quarters reserved for West Indian families. She turned those large breadfruits into breadfruit cou-cou, a food described as a Barbadian comfort food to this day.[88]

This family brought what they knew about gardening and farming from Barbados to the canal. That wisdom provided for them when racist American employers and employment policies—through insufficient compensation, dangerous labor conditions, and inadequate housing—refused to invest in

their survival. Their reclaimed dignity and strength elevated values in relation to communal survival and to Earth itself. Ronica Campbell insists that
she never felt poor. She remembers living very well on the canal. At the time
of her interview, at ninety-two years of age, she gives gratitude and praise to
God that the family always had something to eat. But her regrets center on the
broader West Indian community. Families lived close together and generally
knew one another. She remembers that at the time she believed everyone had
the same thing—enough to eat even when times were hard.

> Now that I am old . . . I know that everybody didn't have, and I used to say
> that if I had known, I would maybe give out something more, because we could
> afford to give, and I would have given more if I had known what I know now,
> now that I am old.[89]

This story of survival, and of the impact that such knowledge could have
had on the broader community, is even more remarkable when placed in
conversation with the controversy surrounding gardening in the West Indian
community at the time. Struggles over gardening, education, and a sense of
their own humanity play an important role in the interrelated understandings
of race, class, gender, and the environment.

Ecocreolization—or agential self-definition arising in response to interrelated violence centered on race, class, gender, and the environment—plays
out in many ways at the site of the Panamá Canal. Debates around the value
of teaching West Indian children to garden or farm offer important insights
to ecowomanist approaches due to the direct linkage of identity with community values about the human relationship to Earth. These debates grew out
of a decades-long struggle over racialization, citizenship, and identity. The
first US period of canal construction ended in 1914, leaving a large number
of West Indian laborers stranded in Panamá or refusing to return home due
to fear of labor shortages. They often lacked the funds to return, and there
were extensive disputes over responsibility for the cost of their repatriation.
Caribbean nations worried about the impact of so many people returning
home in need of work. The Isthmian Canal Commission sought to lessen
the cost of sending laborers home while simultaneously vilifying the impact
of unemployed West Indians refusing to leave Panamá.[90] Cultural conflicts
between Black Panamanian citizens, descended from Spanish enslavement
in the 1500s, and laborers from the Caribbean mirrored national tensions
around continued residency or citizenship for West Indians.[91] The arguments
were cultural, and the dividing line was Castilian Spanish. Ideologies of
eugenics fostered and amplified these tensions, and later shaped Panamanian
constitutional law, which by 1941 stated "Castilian Spanish is the official language of the Republic. It is the function of the state to insure [*sic*] its purity,

conservation, and instruction throughout the country."[92] The 1941 constitution built on a 1926 law that blocked immigration for "negroes whose native language is not Spanish," and went as far as rescinding the citizenship of the children of Black migrants who were born later than 1928.[93]

Disputes over West Indian residency, citizenship, and education were directly tied to issues of labor and identity. Even though many West Indians never returned to their countries of origin and went on to work on the expansion of the canal that began in 1939, Panamá continued to enforce their displacement in place by legally confining them to the area of the Canal Zone. Historian and journalist George Westerman's unpublished manuscript on the lives of West Indians in Panamá notes that while the government went to great lengths to prevent the immigration of more laborers from the Caribbean to build the canal's third set of locks in 1939, it also made provisions to limit the permanent access of those who secured jobs:

> A clause in the contract of the West Indian workers stipulated that they were not supposed to enter into Panamanian territory, as the immigration laws of this country aimed at their exclusion. At the expiration of their contracts, unless renewed, the Canal Zone Government was expected to enforce the repatriation provisions of these workers.[94]

The Isthmian Canal Commission was also responsible for educating West Indian children at the same time.

The Millers's children all mention the high quality of their schools in the Canal Zone. Born in 1918, 1921, and sometime after 1921, these sisters all experienced education in the "colored schools" in the time between the initial US period of canal construction and its expansion in 1939. They had West Indian teachers who offered them a higher level of education than the official eight grades available at their school.[95] Their father worked at the canal for approximately fifty years, so this family was not a part of the waves of repatriation in the early to mid-twentieth century.[96] It is notable that their teachers taught them little Spanish, and they continued to speak little Spanish at the time of their interview in 2011.[97] Historian and theologian Trevor O'Reggio argues convincingly that Canal Zone schools primarily aimed to assimilate West Indian children to their role as laborers separate from the rest of Panamá.

> The Canal Zone schools . . . served as centers of socialization for West Indian children, to inform them about their role in Canal Zone society. The message was clear: West Indian children were to be given a basic education so that they could function as literate laborers. . . . While the education they gave was good, unfortunately, in many cases, it prevented a swift integration into Panamanian

society. The education served to immerse the students in the cultural values of the old country, emphasizing English language skills and British culture without giving sufficient attention to the language and culture of the new country in which the immigrants found themselves.[98]

This reality racialized peoples from the African diaspora based on the horrific irony of relative human worth assigned based on one's colonizers. If your community was ravaged by the Spanish, you had the legal right to citizenship, but if your people were pillaged by the British, your family had few rights and you were required to remain in the ten designated miles of the Canal Zone. A key question in the ability of West Indian children to succeed in Panamá centered on the utility and value of agriculture on the isthmus.

The US Senate engaged questions of the potential for agriculture in Panamá from the beginning of the canal venture. Charles E. Magoon, who served as general counsel for the Isthmian Canal Commission and later as governor of the Canal Zone, testified before the US Senate Committee on Interoceanic Canals in 1906 about low investment in agriculture in Panamá. He details his surprise at the vast areas of undeveloped land, given its fertility. Magoon notes how to a "western man it is a constant aggravation to see that beautiful soil . . . not utilized," explaining the value of corn that he imagines could be cultivated in Panamá.[99] He details the arability of valley, savannah, and plains lands around the Canal Zone. He even classifies the mountain ranges as fertile. He dismisses Indigenous Panamanians as unlikely to undertake agricultural labor in the current generation, but believes that there will be an agricultural population "left over from the employment by the Commission" in the future.[100] Panamanian leadership attempts to realize this vision concurrent with repatriation following the opening of the canal in 1914. Sir Archibald Grenfell Price, a geographer and historian from Australia, reports in his theories on the "color problem" emerging from population increase as early as 1911 among West Indian laborers imported to Panamá by the United States that

> at the end of the [first] construction period, the Government permitted some thousands of West Indian Negroes to attempt agriculture on the shores of Gatún Lake and in other parts of the Canal Zone hoping thus to help dismissed employees, to deal with overpopulation, and to increase supplies for the Zone community.[101]

By 1932, the governor's report bemoans insufficient repatriation, a slump in business-related employment, and the building of infrastructure such as roads between the capital and the interior leading to greater movement of the population from rural areas to the cities.[102] These factors all open up an ongoing debate about the future of farming in Panamá.

Hierarchies of knowledge—including the regular disparagement of West Indian, Indigenous Panamanian, and Chinese methods of gardening or farming in Panamá—shape American approaches to agriculture at the site of the canal. A 1912 report from the US Department of Agriculture's Bureau of Soils and Bureau of Plant Industry dismisses Indigenous Panamanian and West Indian endeavors as "meager," Indigenous Panamanian approaches as "primitive," and Chinese methods as "unsanitary."[103] The report values the efficiency of agriculture based on which tools are used (if any) and how close the cultivated lands are to being planted in neat rows. Such imposition of Western agricultural standards results in assessments that are laughable to the modern reader. In the midst of an assessment of small farms alongside the canal, the report notes the obvious success of their so-called cultural methods:

> Mixed farming, in the sense of growing together a number of different species of plants, is the most common type of agriculture. Frequently a dwelling, usually a palm-thatched shack . . . will, at some distance, be completely hidden from view by a luxuriant tangle of tropical fruits, vegetables, and ornamentals, such as papayas, chayotes, bananas, yams, sugar cane, roselle, antigonon, etc.[104]

The devaluation of non-American approaches as uncultured utterly misses the value of knowledge born from relation to Earth itself. To scorn the knowledge of a household so successful at gardening that their home cannot be seen from a distance due to the immense fecundity of edible plant life surrounding it is nothing less than hubris itself. Such successful labor demonstrates efficient land use and a complex understanding of what is likely to succeed in the impacted ecosystem surrounding the canal.

The report confirms that West Indians like Eldon Miller are working to "cultivate small patches during spare hours from canal work" by 1912.[105] It further demonstrates that American palates serve to discredit so-called cultural farming methods more than the results of such techniques. The writers find the demand for plant-based foods in Panamá "abnormal," and attribute their appeal to "9,000 American and European palates mostly unused to fresh tropical products."[106] The claim is that "palates accustomed to Irish potatoes, lettuce, cabbage, and garden peas do not readily adjust themselves to yams, taniers, chayotes, and similar tropical vegetables which satisfy the tropical palate."[107] As a result, the canal commissary imports the vast majority of its agricultural products from the United States, and the abundance of tropical foods is rarely served in the dining halls, hotels, or private homes of white Americans in Panamá. Yet still, the official governmental recommendation is for heavy manual labor to be done by West Indian and "tropical" workers under the leadership of white supervisors hailing from temperate zones.[108] Farms operated in this manner are to utilize "better strains of staple crops as have already demonstrated their adaptability to the conditions," and find more efficient methods to "replace the wild and intractable native vegetation of the present shack-farm agriculture."[109]

Once again the official recommendation is to tame the wilderness and to force plant life preferred by white palates to adapt to the environment of the tropics, rather than questioning the gardening methods of white residents who arrive in the Canal Zone with no lived experience of surviving in the tropics. The logics of colonization remain on full display in the years of canal construction. Interestingly, these recommendations conclude with a call for West Indian children to be taught gardening in Canal Zone schools. The authors' belief is that "the rising generation would in this way be brought into touch with such advances as are made, and would gradually acquire the new point of view and intelligent interest in rational and progressive agricultural methods."[110] Yet in 2011, at ninety-two years of age, Ronica Campbell still dreams of the high quality of her father's yams.[111]

It is in the next generation of West Indians at the canal, in the children of the migrants, that we see the full impact of relation to Earth in self-definition and the concern for human dignity. In debates over the content of the curriculum in West Indian schools between the two US periods of canal construction, community leaders struggled over the relative worth of gardening in the curriculum. Some felt that too much of their children's education focused on agriculture when there were few agricultural jobs in the urban and suburban areas that housed the majority of the community. Others believed there would be significant future opportunities for agricultural work.[112] Yet the gardening taught in schools at the time still focused on crops more suitable to climates further north. The *Annual Reports of the Canal Zone Experiment Gardens for the Fiscal Years 1935 and 1936* reports the types of fruits and vegetables cultivated as an aid to school gardens.[113] Such gardens are identified as only existing in schools for the children of silver roll employees, and the primary crops listed are grown with irrigation during the dry season. Very little is recommended in terms of working with the particular benefits of Panamá's natural environment. All plants are described in terms of their ability to adapt to the climate.[114] Neo-imperialism appropriates the labor of plants themselves to the task of cultural imperialism through the availability of food at the Canal Zone.

Understanding oneself in connection to Earth, despite the tangle of racialized categories, gender norms, and violating labor practices, provides an opportunity for rehumanization at all levels. In response to colonial legacies and the practices of neo-imperialism, the process of ecocreolization offers dignity, agency, and self-definition to communities facing multiple violations of oppression and forced displacement. Connection to Earth itself offers an unassailable strength that persists across generations. Olive Senior emphasizes that

> kitchen gardens, bush living, or farming—any escape to more natural surroundings—was also of profound psychological significance. . . . A cultivated plot could be an anchor. . . . In conditions of uncertainty and transience, a piece of ground provided not just food but spiritual nourishment. It also provided a space apart from prying eyes in which men and women could worship as they pleased, summoning the deities or the ancestors to intercede in times of affliction, offering spiritual protection otherwise, a space for ritual worship and healing. All these were important elements of the West Indian cosmos, the touchstone of belief systems partly derived from Africa, which required not a church building but a ritually prepared space in which one's feet could touch bare earth and the gods and ancestors could be summoned.[115]

Inherited environmental culture persists, as is seen in the Miller family's recollections. Dedicated labor, skill at gardening and farming, and skill at turning a variety of plant life into healthy food for the family all lead to a sense of well-being and fulfillment in daily life. Supposedly uncultured growing practices, in relation to Earth, provide for family and even the broader community. Their knowledge of self in relation to Earth blesses the Miller family with a sense of ingenuity rather than the force-fed, dehumanizing lies offered by the Americans. For a family that migrated to Panamá to do the manual labor of canal construction and that, two generations later, had a family member captaining the boats as they moved through the canal, the transgenerational teaching that the children "reap the sweets of it" (all the labor, sacrifice, and retention of the good in the face of such evils) is nothing short of wisdom.[116] It is to inherited environmental practices themselves that ecowomanism must turn for rehumanizing ways of knowing in relation to Earth—for the construction of ecowomanist earth epistemologies that might serve to heal relationships damaged over multiple generations.

NOTES

1. Margarita Vargas-Betancourt, "Finding the Silver Voice: Afro-Antilleans in the Panama Canal Museum Collection at the University of Florida" (paper presented at the 13th International Conference on Caribbean Literature, "Panama in the Caribbean: The Caribbean in Panama," University of Panama, Panama City, November 13–16, 2013).

2. Nixon, *Slow Violence*, 19–20, 164.

3. John McGroarty, M. H. Walsh, and J. K. Baxter, *Macwalbax: A Collection of Poems, Cartoons, and Comment* (Panama City: The Panama Times, 1926), front inside cover.

4. McGroarty, Walsh, and Baxter, *Macwalbax*, front inside cover.

5. Nelson Rounsevell, *The Life Story of N.R., or 40 Years of Rambling, Gambling and Publishing* (Panama City: Panama American Publishing Co., 1933), 164.

6. McGroarty, Walsh, and Baxter, *Macwalbax*, 7.

7. McGroarty, Walsh, and Baxter, 7.

8. Rounsevell, *Life Story of N.R.*, 147.

9. Rounsevell, *Life Story of N.R.*, 150.

10. Rounsevell, *Life Story of N.R.*, 147.

11. Sue Core and Ann Cordts McKeown, *Isthmiana* (Panama City: Panama American Publishing Company, 1939), 2.

12. Rounsevell, *Life Story of N.R.*, 146.

13. Rounsevell, McKeown146.

14. McGroarty, Walsh, and Baxter, *Macwalbax*, 4–6.

15. Senior, *Dying to Better Themselves*, 140–41, 206, 234–35, 240.

16. Senior, *Dying to Better Themselves,* 240.

17. Krista A. Thompson, *An Eye for the Tropics: Tourism, Photography, and Framing the Caribbean Picturesque* (Durham, NC: Duke University Press, 2006), 103.

18. Thompson, *An Eye for the Tropics,* 102, 104.

19. Thompson, *An Eye for the Tropics,* 103, 106.

20. Thompson, *An Eye for the Tropics,* 106–07.

21. Thompson, *An Eye for the Tropics,* 106–10.

22. For Jacob Frank Coonley's "On the Way to Market," see https://nagb.org.bs/mixedmediablog/2017/8/21/from-the-collection-on-the-way-to-market-ca-1877-78-by-jacob-f-coonley. For Winslow Homer's "On the Way to Market," see https://www.brooklynmuseum.org/opencollection/objects/94858.

23. McGroarty, Walsh, and Baxter, "Carnival Days," in *Macwalbax*, 122–23.

24. McGroarty, Walsh, and Baxter, "Carnival Days," 122–23.

25. McGroarty, Walsh, and Baxter, "Panama's Market Place," in *Macwalbax*, 110.

26. McGroarty, Walsh, and Baxter, "Panama's Market Place," 110.

27. McGroarty, Walsh, and Baxter, "The Wash Lady," in *Macwalbax*, 46.

28. My wise Jamaican grandmother, Carmen Lynton Holt, tellingly used to call blonde hair and blue eyes "nature's passport."

29. McGroarty, Walsh, and Baxter, "The Wash Lady," 46.

30. McGroarty, Walsh, and Baxter, "The Wash Lady," 47.

31. McGroarty, Walsh, and Baxter, "The Wash Lady," 47.

32. McGroarty, Walsh, and Baxter, "The Wash Lady," 47.

33. McGroarty, Walsh, and Baxter, "The Wash Lady," 46.

34. Rivas, *El trabajo de las mujeres*, 154–55.

35. Joan Flores-Villalobos, "'Freak Letters': Tracing Gender, Race, and Diaspora in the Panama Canal Archive," *Small Axe* 23, no. 2 (July 2019): 40, https://doi.org/10.1215/07990537-7703266.

36. McGroarty, Walsh, and Baxter, "The Wash Lady," 47.

37. McGroarty, Walsh, and Baxter, "The Banana Lady," in *Macwalbax*, 48.

38. McGroarty, Walsh, and Baxter, "The Banana Lady," 48.

39. McGroarty, Walsh, and Baxter, "The Banana Lady," 48.

40. McGroarty, Walsh, and Baxter, "The Banana Lady," 48.

41. McGroarty, Walsh, and Baxter, "The Banana Lady," 48.

42. Frenkel, "Jungle Stories," 317–18; Greenberg, *Manifest Manhood*, 78.

43. Ruth Y. Jenkins, "The Gaze of the Victorian Woman Traveler," in *Gender, Genre, and Identity in Women's Travel Writing*, ed. Kristi Siegel (New York: Peter Lang, 2004), 15–16, 19.

44. Joyce E. Kelley, *Excursions into Modernism: Women Writers, Travel, and the Body* (Burlington, VT: Ashgate, 2015), 23–26, 50–53.

45. Chu-Chueh Cheng, "Frances Trollope's America and Anna Leonowen's Siam," in *Gender, Genre, and Identity*, ed. Siegel, 123–24.

46. Senior, *Dying to Better Themselves*, 242.

47. Scholars occasionally cite Elizabeth Kittredge Parker as a primary source for life on the canal, but a close read of *Panama Canal Bride* has not been published to date.

48. Parker, *Panama Canal Bride*, 9.

49. Parker, *Panama Canal Bride*, 9–10.

50. Parker, *Panama Canal Bride*, 12.

51. Parker, *Panama Canal Bride*, 15.

52. Parker, *Panama Canal Bride*, 15–16.

53. Parker, *Panama Canal Bride*, 17.

54. Parker, *Panama Canal Bride*, 17.

55. Parker, *Panama Canal Bride*, 19.

56. Parker, *Panama Canal Bride*, 19, 21.

57. Parker, *Panama Canal Bride*, 21.

58. Parker, *Panama Canal Bride*, 21–24.

59. Parker, *Panama Canal Bride*, 27.

60. Parker, *Panama Canal Bride*, 30–31.

61. Parker, *Panama Canal Bride*, 31.

62. Parker, *Panama Canal Bride*, 34.

63. Parker, *Panama Canal Bride*, 35–36.

64. Parker, *Panama Canal Bride*, 36–37.

65. Parker, *Panama Canal Bride*, 37.

66. Parker, *Panama Canal Bride*, 37.

67. Parker, *Panama Canal Bride*, 37.

68. Parker, *Panama Canal Bride*, 37.

69. Parker, *Panama Canal Bride*, 39–40.

70. Parker, *Panama Canal Bride*, 85.

71. Parker, *Panama Canal Bride*, 84–85.

72. Parker, *Panama Canal Bride*, 40.

73. Parker, *Panama Canal Bride*, 90.

74. Ronice Campbell (pseudonym), interview by Alison Saunders, June 30, 2011, MP3 video.

75. Christina Smith, "Saunders Makes History with 'Panama Dreams,'" *Loop Barbados*, March 23, 2018, http://www.loopnewsbarbados.com/content/saunders -makes-history-panama-dreams.

76. "'Panama Dreams'—A Documentary by Alison Saunders," interview by TTT Live Online, September 19, 2019, video, 6:35, https://www.youtube.com/watch ?v=pUUSi0Dytx0.

77. Campbell, interview.

78. Irie Davis (pseudonym), interview by Alison Saunders, June 30, 2011, MP3 video.

79. Kady Grant (pseudonym), interview by Alison Saunders, June 30, 2011, MP3 video.

80. Davis, interview.

81. Davis, interview.

82. Greene, *Canal Builders*, 62–69.

83. Campbell, interview.

84. Campbell, interview.

85. Davis, interview.

86. Davis, interview.

87. Campbell, interview.

88. Melanie Weekes and Kimberly Bourne, "Cooking Bajan Style: Breadfruit Cou-Cou," *The Blog, Loop Barbados*, January 8, 2014, https://loopbarbados.com/ loop-blog/cooking-bajan-style-breadfruit-cou-cou.

89. Campbell, interview.

90. Greene, *Canal Builders*, 339–42.

91. Trevor O'Reggio, *Between Alienation and Citizenship: The Evolution of Black West Indian Society in Panama 1914–1964* (Lanham, MD: University Press of America, 2006), 34–35.

92. Melva Lowe de Goodin, *People of African Ancestry in Panama 1501–2012* (Panamá City: Imprenta Sibauste, 2014), 89–92.

93. Lara Putnam, "Eventually Alien: The Multigenerational Saga of West Indians in Central America 1870–1940," in *Blacks & Blackness in Central America: Between Race and Place*, ed. Lowell Gudmundson and Justin Wolfe (Durham, NC: Duke University Press, 2010), 290.

94. George Westerman, "Fifty Years of West Indian Life on the Isthmus of Panama" (unpublished manuscript, typescript), George Westerman Collection (MG505 101/1), Schomburg Center for Research in Black Culture, New York Public Library, 134.

95. Campbell, interview.

96. Davis, interview.

97. Grant, interview.

98. O'Reggio, *Between Alienation and Citizenship*, 71–72.

99. *Investigation of Panama Canal Matters*, 696, 805–06.

100. *Investigation of Panama Canal Matters*, 806.

101. Archibald Grenfell Price, *White Settlers in the Tropics* (New York: American Geographical Society, 1939), 165–66.

102. Price, *White Settlers in the Tropics*, 165–66.

103. Hugh H. Bennett and Wm. A. Taylor, *The Agricultural Possibilities of the Canal Zone*, parts 1–2, prepared for the US Department of Agriculture, Office of the Secretary, Bureau of Soils and Bureau of Plant Industry (Washington, DC: Government Printing Office, 1912), 11–12, https://ufdc.ufl.edu/AA00029633/00001.

104. Bennett and Taylor, *Agricultural Possibilities*, 12.

105. Bennett and Taylor, *Agricultural Possibilities*, 19.

106. Bennett and Taylor, *Agricultural Possibilities*, 43.

107. Bennett and Taylor, *Agricultural Possibilities*, 43.

108. Bennett and Taylor, *Agricultural Possibilities*, 45.

109. Bennett and Taylor, *Agricultural Possibilities*, 47.

110. Bennett and Taylor, *Agricultural Possibilities*, 49.

111. Campbell, interview.

112. Westerman, "Fifty Years of West Indian Life," 181–83.

113. *Annual Reports of the Canal Zone Experiment Gardens for the Fiscal Years 1935 and 1936* (Mount Hope, Canal Zone: Panama Canal Press, 1939), 26–31.

114. *Annual Reports of the Canal Zone Experiment Gardens,* 26–31.

115. Senior, *Dying to Better Themselves*, 264.

116. Campbell, interview.

Chapter 4

Dignity and Striving

An Ecowomanist Moral Anthropology

Ecowomanism undoubtedly benefits from incorporating inherited environmental cultures and identity development into womanism's well-established work to dismantle race, gender, and class oppression. The integration of Jacqueline Grant's early work to bring the broader context of imperialism into a womanist framework (see chapter 2) allows for decolonizing analyses that are crucial to constructing environmental ethics in our current context of environmental devastation. The resulting knowledge gained from the study of ecocreolization (as defined in chapters 1 and 3) provides critical breadth to the work of environmental ethics. Yet ecowomanism as a methodology further requires engagement with foundational questions of personhood and human nature in this time when the urgency of earth justice pushes many scholars to seek beyond human categories and identity (and, unfortunately, agency and the perpetual evil of dehumanization) in an attempt to dismantle the destructive power of anthropocentrism. We are once again called to tell our stories in environmental time. Ecowomanism requires not only a reclamation of inherited environmental cultures, but further necessitates an unflinching examination of systems of oppression as a corrective to what Val Plumwood identifies as master narratives of dominance and globalization, thereby allowing movement toward the construction of decolonizing, diasporic, multireligious environmental ethics as an ecowomanist approach to the problem of environmental destruction.[1]

This chapter specifically aims toward an ecowomanist moral anthropology to reclaim the value of that which is considered human in the work of environmental ethics. It nevertheless remains cognizant of the destructive powers of the Anthropocene[2] and does so through the embrace of a diasporic multireligious epistemology. This chapter builds its moral anthropology in conversation with the writings of Beverly Mitchell that theorize human nature as human dignity before God in the face of unimaginable suffering;[3] Delores Williams's examination of the interrelated vilification of Black women's bodies and Earth;[4] Monique Allewaert's construction of agential personhood through the engagement of fractured bodies and colonized Earth;[5] and Anna Peterson's work to understand the embodiment, relationality, culturality, and territoriality of our human natures as limited by our dependence on the delicate balance of Earth's ecosystems.[6] In a time when we must ask ourselves not how we might save Earth but rather how we are obliged to retain our humaneness in the face of Earth's destruction, justice defines our moral center. If we would retain the best of our humanity in this time of devastation, we must draw on what we know of justice to center our responses to incomprehensible adversity. We are already seeing unimaginable hardship and suffering that will mark the coming years. The question is: How do we wish to live through such challenging times?

Ecowomanist approaches offer particular gifts of knowledge transmission and recovery that ground our understanding of humanity in relation to Earth. Ecowomanism encounters environmental destruction in its clearest form as a colonial legacy. A decolonizing ecowomanist ethic therefore requires moral wisdom predicated on an understanding of deterritorialization and displacement—one that is inherently diasporic. In ecocreolization lies a particular knowing that serves to interrupt enslaving experiences of the disaster that is to come. We are called instead to face our destructive future with a vision of justice—earth justice.

This chapter addresses womanist Earth-honoring epistemologies by proposing the reclamation of diasporic practices collectively labeled as *Obeah* for the identification of cultural inheritances and knowledge production that offer agency, accountability, and a material grounding in the natural world. Rather than a central theology, this chapter engages magic as an inherited environmental culture through the traditions and practices of Obeah. This approach allows for the exploration of a multireligious, intercultural, creolized response to the devastation. It is inherently pluralistic and unswayed by hierarchies of identity that too often dehumanize the most vulnerable among us. Obeah offers rich potential for developing emergent transnational ecowomanist ethics in that it contains material interventions that extend spiritual accountability at the level of death and dying, thus expanding our knowledge of what it means to be human within an earth community.

Obeah represents not only a set of inherited practices, but further offers spiritual covenant. It offers us covenants with teeth, sometimes literally.[7] It empowers a cycle that some might label magic and many demonize through negative stereotypes of witchcraft. I suggest that we approach Obeah as a power to call into account and to reconcile environmental (and other forms of) desecration. Obeah serves as an embodied ethic whose materiality extends to the natural world and the context in which we find ourselves. It not only provides a personal system of morality in the face of competing values but also has the further potential to anchor intracommunal accountability, as witnessed during various slave rebellions and other reclamations of human agency (see "Obeah as Diasporic Religious Epistemology"). Its very efficacy within an otherwise disempowered community was a central motivation for the vilification of Obeah by outside colonizing and enslaving cultures. This chapter honors Obeah as a diasporic multireligious epistemology whose knowledge production can be used to understand our human nature in relation to Earth. It is not a call to romanticize magic in a way that will miraculously erase centuries of human evils. Instead, it is an invitation to engage an agential spiritual materialism across a range of spiritual practices that return the wisdom of ancestry winnowed through the fires of generational suffering as a way of our mothers' "making do."

Obeah is a power to be approached with caution—not because of its alleged evil but because of its insistence that we learn responsibly in the community. I am not suggesting that we take alligators' teeth to hand to right the wrongs of the Anthropocene. I am claiming the need to learn from what alligators' teeth, and birds' eggs, and a bit of soil out of place have to teach us. I am insisting that we honor and uplift our elders who have passed this knowledge between the generations, creating epistemologies of resistance and accountability at great personal risk. Can Obeah be misused? Certainly. Any power can be misused. We see that throughout the human history. And yet we must reject the outside devaluation of the wisdom of our grandmothers in the name of religious propriety. Let forced assimilation be known as dehumanization, and the inherited values and cultural expressions that keep us in step with the broader earth community return to their place in the sun.

ECOWOMANISM, MORAL ANTHROPOLOGY, AND THE NEED FOR NEW EPISTEMIC APPROACHES

In his paradigm-changing work *The Future of Ethics*, environmental ethicist Willis Jenkins redefines the ground on which we approach the immensity of climate disruption. This scholar, known for his encouragement to reimagine our theological traditions in light of what we now know about environmental destruction, states plainly that we are in a state of "moral incompetence" when it comes to climate change. He argues that our religious traditions and theological teachings were refined in an era that could not conceive of the Anthropocene.[8] Climate disruption is an example of what Jenkins describes as an "unprecedented problem." He writes that the greatest peril of climate change [is] that the accidental powers of humanity generate problems that exceed our moral imagination and defeat our abilities to take responsibility. Insofar as atmospheric powers escape the bounds of justice or make talk of loving neighbors unintelligible, they disinherit cultures of the concepts and practices that sustain a way of being human.[9]

While Jenkins makes a convincing argument that religious traditions developed in a time when humanity could not conceive of the Anthropocene, I believe there remains utility in religious teachings born of dignity and strength in the face of incomprehensible evil. It is to those traditions that we turn—not to avoid what we have wrought, but as a way to carry the best of our being forward through the suffering that is yet to come.

Womanist thought has enormous potential to expand Jenkins's apt characterization of the moral landscape. In her work on the lives of English-speaking women of the Caribbean, cultural critic and poet Olive Senior explores the primary familial value of "making do." By this, she means the common cultural understanding that for poor women in the Caribbean "making something out of nothing" is fundamental to family survival and teaches us the primary values of "resourcefulness, endurance, and sacrifice."[10] This is just one example of many drawn from the wisdom of our mothers' mothers, teaching us to maintain our agency, prioritize our families and communities, and "make do" that we might survive. We see this central moral teaching expanded to an explicitly womanist source of transgenerational power, agency, and reclamation of self in relation to all of creation in womanist theologian Karen Baker-Fletcher's work on the life and thought of Anna Julia Cooper.[11] It is further refined in the scholarship of womanist theologian Monica Coleman, and ecowomanists logically expand that inherited knowledge to environmental thought.[12] An ecowomanist ethic calls us to expand our notions of family, care, relationality, sustainability, and endurance to bring the strength of a people that survived and maintained their dignity through unprecedented violence and violation alongside multiple experiences of displacement to the problem of environmental devastation. There are important lessons to be learned from those who survived the shattering of everything that they knew and held dear. Questions examining our understanding of human nature are intimately tied to religious concepts of human relatedness and responsibility to the natural world. An ecowomanist ethic, particularly one that seeks to address the historical abuses and lingering religious ideologies of human dominion that pollute attempts at collaboration between the Global North and the Global South, must therefore seek to define a womanist understanding of humanity within the larger earth community.

Ecowomanism, drawn in large part from lived experiences of unexpected solutions to inhumane problems, impacts something as unimaginably large as climate disruption and environmental decay by recentering that which we have driven to the margins for so long that we assume its abnormality (see chapter 2). Inherited environmental cultures matter profoundly to the earth justice-seeking behavioral changes that theological exploration has so far struggled to catalyze in our communities of faith. At stake in these life lessons and in the comparative value, they receive within our theoethical constructions the repossession of moral wisdom that troubles the legacies of chattel slavery and colonialism lying at the heart of logics of ownership, entitlement, and environmentally destructive behaviors. This approach rejects all romanticized imaginary returns to an Edenic era predating the violation of our moral covenant with creation. Instead, it explores moral pluralism as a decolonial response. We allow the continuation of dominant cultures of rapacious global consumption at our peril. A methodology of reclaiming inherited environmental cultures in the quest to center justice in living out the best of our human nature requires the wisdom of all of our grandmothers. In our diverse ethnic identities, even those so silenced by mythologies of whiteness as to seem lost to the tides of history, there exist relationships to nonhuman nature that predate settler colonial worldviews, resource theft and control, abhorrent religious justifications for enslavement, and the imposition of colonized and otherized identities. It is these lasting stories, many of which masquerade as unexplained family traditions (those things that are educated out of us in the name of progress or success), that might serve to ground an ecowomanist moral anthropology and release us from the environmental apathy of the day.

As a corrective to environmental apathy, Jenkins's scholarship invites us to moral creativity as a site of hope and investment. He identifies engaging problems as an act of faith in a transcendent and transforming God as an important, though not required, practice that inspires moral creativity.[13] He also calls for us to work with strangers—to cross borders and boundaries of identity, disciplines, and tradition—in order to invest in shared projects and foster cooperation. This is a moral obligation for those of us who participate in what he names as "globalizing networks of power that exceed the reach of our moral and political memberships."[14] Jenkins calls for us to work from below. His investment and faith in moral creativity born, in part, of faith in the transcendent naturally aligns with Mayra Rivera's postcolonial theology where transcendence can be found within creation itself.[15]

Rivera draws on the corpus of Latin American liberation theology, and the work of Ignacio Ellacuría in particular, to argue for a transcendent God whose transcendence crosses *into* human history rather than away from it. Responding to common criticisms of liberation theologies as reducing transcendence to "mere" social action, Rivera instead describes what we commonly hear as a preferential option—whether for the poor, the otherized, or even Earth—as the transcendence of a God that can be found within the open wounds of the world but perfectly free from its oppressions.[16] It is this possibility, this justice-seeking invitation to a godly and salvific gaze, that holds the depth of promise and possibility that we seek in response to environmental destruction. If we can experience the slight touch of transcendence in solidarity with the suffering of the world, then surely the same touches grace the wisdom that allowed our grandmothers to survive such injury; surely the same touches grace the wisdom of our grandmothers whose knowledge was not intended as a platform to enslave, colonize, or control Earth.

JUSTICE AT THE FOUNDATIONS OF ECOWOMANIST THOUGHT

Womanist scholars rightly return to the definition of womanism in the preface of Alice Walker's *In Search of Our Mothers' Gardens* for the central ontological assumptions of a working womanist methodology.[17] Ecowomanism further benefits from a closer read of Walker's entire corpus. Walker's antinuclear speech, in particular, "Only Justice Can Stop a Curse," provides critical material for an unflinching ecowomanist response to the intersection of colonial legacies of destruction on both Earth and women of the African diaspora. In her speech, Walker cites a curse-prayer that Zora Neale Hurston recorded during her anthropological studies in the 1920s. Walker reports that this invocation was old when Hurston first collected it, and further illustrates the likelihood that a woman of color, "starved, enslaved, humiliated, and carelessly trampled to death," was likely the first to pray this curse.[18] It is difficult to argue with her assertion that these intentions, heightened by the suffering prayers of generations, are finally coming to pass.

To the Man God: O Great One, I have been sorely tried by my enemies and have been blasphemed and lied against. My good thoughts and my honest actions have been turned to bad actions and dishonest ideas. My home has been ill-treated. My dear ones have been backbitten and their virtue questioned. O Man God, I beg that this that I ask for my enemies shall come to pass:

That the South wind shall scorch their bodies and make them wither and shall not be tempered to them. That the North wind shall freeze their blood and numb their muscles and that it shall not be tempered to them. That the West wind shall blow away their life's breath and will not leave their hair grow, and that their fingernails shall fall off and their bones shall crumble. That the East wind shall make their minds grow dark, their sight shall fall and their seed dry up so that they shall not multiply.

I ask that their fathers and mothers from their furthest generation will not intercede for them before the great throne, and that the wombs of their women shall not bear fruit except for strangers, and that they shall become extinct. I pray that the children who may come shall be weak of mind and paralyzed of limb and that they themselves shall curse them in their turn for ever turning the breath of life into their bodies. I pray that disease and death shall be forever with them and that their worldly goods shall not prosper, and that their crops shall not multiply and that their cows, their sheep, and their hogs and all the living beasts shall die of starvation and thirst. I pray that their house shall be unroofed and that the rain, the thunder and lightning shall find the innermost recesses of their home and that the foundation shall crumble and the floods tear it asunder. I pray that the sun shall not shed its rays on them in benevolence, but instead it shall beat down on them and burn them and destroy them. I pray that the moon shall not give them peace, but instead shall deride them and decry them and cause their minds to shrivel. I pray that their friends shall betray them and cause them loss of power, of gold and of silver, and that their enemies shall smite them until they beg for mercy which shall not be given them. I pray that their tongues shall forget how to speak in sweet words, and that it shall be paralyzed and that all about them shall be desolation, pestilence and death. O Man God, I ask you for all these things because they have dragged me in the dust and destroyed my good name; broken my heart and caused me to curse the day that I was born. So be it.[19]

The language in this curse prayer that invokes disability as punishment before God is in no way an intention that one would advocate within an ecowomanist frame. This text carries within it ableist notions of wholeness and holiness that must not be carried forward into a present-day analysis. Walker ends on her intention to protect Earth as her home. She responds to a centuries-old, blood-soaked prayer with a fearless call for justice. In her admitted resonance with this curse -prayer, and her heartfelt choice to respond to it with the courage to lean into hope and justice, Walker offers us a way forward through the snarled consequences of rapacious settler colonialism and chattel slavery. Her fearlessness requires the audacity to center the promise of our full humanity in response.

One might respond to the curse-prayer with a renewed intention: *Oh my best beloveds. You to whom my libations are offered; you whose absence is grieved in each moment of celebration; each passage marked; each baby dedicated; each love experienced, celebrated, or lost. You cherished ones whose perseverance I wear as flesh. No more shall my skin, teeth, bones, muscle, and mind be used as a human shield to justify colonizing and enslaving evils. No longer shall the legacies I bear at a cellular level (coded in the very chains of my DNA—blessed and glorious as your contributions to*

*it may be) serve to anaesthetize me to the movement of your spilled blood,
your unremarked bones, your unrelenting agency cascading down through
histories of unimaginable suffering.*

*Did they/we/I believe we could violate the core matter of all existence—
rending flesh, reducing humanity, remaining aloof to the tides of evil—without draining the very planet (Mater, Matter, Materia) of all goodness and
all life?*

We be flesh and bone and loss and the very promise of beauty.

We be ontologies of power born of our ancestors.

*For the cellular offerings of all those in the centuries-long violation of
personhood run through my veins. And therefore magic and might, validation
and violation, capacity and corruption all define my inheritance. We too must
"make do" with this legacy. How many have prayed this curse into being as
their blood fertilized the soil? How many daughters regret(ted) their birth?
How many mothers fear(ed) for their children?*

*Our words come into being as a prayer answered in its own time. Of all
that has been taught to us of our human living, what will shape our days in
the suffering that has already come? How* can *justice stop a curse?*

OBEAH AS DIASPORIC RELIGIOUS EPISTEMOLOGY

Obeah, by virtue of its creolized and diasporic evolutions, transmits wisdom
from various peoples and lineages through forced migration and into the construction of new communities and racialized identities. The intentional sen-
sationalism and false stereotypes of Obeah created by European men seeking
to redefine, conscribe, and control the bodies of enslaved and colonized Black
women must not undermine the reclamation of Obeah for the construction
of new ways of knowing.[20] Racism, colonizing mindsets, and the ravages of
chattel slavery lie at the heart of European historical assumptions around the
practices collectively (and anthropologically) known as Obeah. In contrast,
inherited cultural values of the African diaspora guide this transformation of
religious traditions and cultural legacies in order to meet the needs and lived
realities born of forced migrations and displacement. Such ways of knowing
grant a type of agency inherently damaging to chattel slavery and to a colonized worldview. On June 5, 2019, *Jamaica Beacon* reported that officials
have finally begun the process of decriminalizing Obeah.[21] It should come as
no surprise that the practices collectively categorized as Obeah have been so
vilified throughout history that they remain policed today by some of the very
communities from which they emerged.[22]

Scholars frequently describe Obeah as a collective set of African-derived
or African-influenced practices, with some debate over the dividing line

between magic and religion, which draw on the supernatural to effect change. Negative terms associated with narrow views of witchcraft dominate the field, while many authors simply echo the writings of early twentieth-century white male anthropologists who universally describe Obeah as evil or demonic. The writings of Jesuit missionary and anthropologist Joseph J. Williams particularly influence this perspective.[23] Williams, writing from the historical accounts of English-born Jamaican historian Edward Long in the 1770s,[24] describes Obeah as the practices of "those whose hoary heads, and something particularly harsh and diabolic in their aspect, together with some skill in plants of the medicinal and poisonous species, have qualified them for successful imposition upon the weak and credulous."[25] Obeah for Williams derives directly from Africans violently transported to Jamaican (and other Caribbean) plantations. His descriptions of Obeah regularly focus on the supposed lack of intellect in those so gullible as to believe in "witchcraft, second-sight, and other pretended supernatural gifts," and those forcibly displaced or creolized Africans whose predatory lack of morality allows them to exploit such gullibility. His writings highlight racist assumptions that inferior intellect and lack of cultural depth are the sole explanations for why Obeah might appeal to those living in the African diaspora.[26]

This categorization is simply one more reflection of a European imaginary maligning non-European cultural values and sources of agential power. Afro-Caribbean religions scholar Dianne M. Stewart describes the almost fetishized supposition that evil is inherent to religions from the African continent as an intentional investment in what she terms "Afrophobia." This too often further becomes a type of internalized oppression where people living in the African diaspora internalize Eurocentric biases as truth and divorce themselves from their own inherited cultures.[27] This same internalized oppression around the use and practice of Obeah can be seen in Panamá following the time of canal construction in the voice of prominent West Indian journalist Albert E. Bell, who, writing for *The Panama American* in 1926, negatively characterized Obeah as both sorcery and necromancy. Bell disparages the practices of Obeah, complaining that the "lack-brains" of his society credit all aspects of their lives to its influences. He grieves that

> the fancies and practices [that] originated with the witch doctors of darkest Africa and today in these enlightened times and places this blight on civilization still exists among our people. To some of them it is life and death, food and drink, the cause of success or failure, their all in all—their God.[28]

While Bell's understanding of Obeah can easily be labeled as internalized Afrophobia, it serves to highlight the strength and persistence of Obeah in the West Indian community of Panamá at the time.

In order to consider Obeah as a collection of inherited environmental cultures functioning at the Panamá Canal during its construction, it is critical to engage Obeah at the times and places of its formation. The historical record begins to identify and document Obeah in the mid- to late eighteenth century, when its role in the fomentation and success of slave rebellions caused planters to take it seriously as a threat against the hegemonic norms of plantation life. Early European documentation focuses primarily on male practitioners, particularly in their connection to uprisings. Black women are mentioned, but mainly as healers or poisoners, not as primary leaders. Legal proceedings and anthropological texts track a European preoccupation with the power granted through Obeah practices, and the ability of these practices to catalyze communal accountability and enhance survival. As the norms of chattel slavery shift through abolition and emancipation in the nineteenth century, the need to treat the Black woman's body as something other than disposable causes planters to focus their attention on Obeah women. These shifting lenses through which Obeah is analyzed by the European gaze nevertheless depict a range of influences that impacted those traveling to work on the Panamá Canal during the economic hardship of the early twentieth century.

While the practices of Obeah are generally attributed to transplanted African cultures by the anthropologists of that era, they evolved in creolized forms as cultures and peoples came together through a shared experience of violation and displacement.[29] The vast majority of creolized communities and cultures forming in the Caribbean due to forced migration and enslavement would later become the same communities transplanted to Panamá for economic reasons following emancipation.[30] Further, the practices of those returning home following the completion of canal construction increased the use of Obeah in their communities of origin.[31] Both directions of migration and displacement illustrate the working of Obeah in the diasporic community that gathered to construct the Panamá Canal. Their resilience and survival in the face of the unimaginable recommend Obeah as a credible example of ecocreolization—what I have termed an agential self-definition in response to the slow violence of imperialism through environmental devastation, forced migration, and racialized violence. Ecocreolization calls for the reclamation of inherited environmental cultures that empowered our mothers to "make do."

Like Stewart, historical anthropologists Jerome Handler and Kenneth Bilby define Obeah by its record of vilification, stating that "for whites, 'Obeah' became a catch-all term for a range of supernatural-related ideas and behaviors that were not of European origin and which they heavily criticized and condemned."[32] Handler and Bilby work to reclaim Obeah from a limited hegemonic narrative through legal and etymological analyses that seek to classify Obeah within the values of the cultural contexts from which its practices emerged. The historical record highlights the usage of the term *Obeah* in the English-speaking Caribbean as early as the beginning of the eighteenth century, aligning these practices with witchcraft and conjuring, bewitchment, trickery, and control.[33] Yet further research, intentionally distanced from long-standing European narratives surrounding Obeah, illustrates a range of broader worldviews. Stewart offers an agential understanding of Obeah, one that situates its communal importance in a post-emancipation context. Stewart "reframe[s] Obeah as a protean institutional structure encompassing ethnic and Pan-African religious cultures, which co-author an African-derived understanding of mystical power as the capacity to use energy dynamically."[34] Such an organically multireligious, intercultural influence can be understood as that which reauthorized (and rehumanized) those whose ability to hold one another and the broader society accountable had been utterly violated by the realities of enslavement, and further as a collection of inherited environmental cultures granting both agency and a deeper understanding of the self.

While several African languages have antecedents to the term *Obeah* that connote definitions of power and witchcraft, they also retain both neutral and positive meanings for the term. The words signify healing skills, and the holding of esoteric knowledge.[35] White enslavers in Jamaica admitted to the superior efficacy of medical treatment from Obeah practitioners over their own medical doctors.[36] Even the appallingly racist Joseph J. Williams concedes the existence of

> really marvelous "Bush remedies." For example, a throbbing headache is quickly relieved by the application of a particular cactus which is split and bound on the forehead; and a severe fever is broken effectively by a "bush tea" known only to the old woman who gathers them, and whose only explanation is "Jes seben bush, Sah, me pick dem one one."[37]

It would be easy to relegate the practices of Obeah across history and cultures to the role of the herbalist whose phytochemical knowledge provides ease and healing. It is more difficult to reconcile with Obeah as it draws on supernatural forces to enact change. Yet in so doing, Obeah has the potential to rehumanize entire communities.

Notably, the term *Obeah* regularly refers to creolized practices, born of an intertwined experience of multiple enslaved peoples bringing their inherited knowledge, spirit, and wisdom into the same spaces of rupture, alongside an insidious and controlling enslaving and settler colonial mindset that thinks nothing of violating large groups of individuals, in part through isolation and the intentional separation of those who share ethnic and cultural identities. As anthropologist Aisha Khan notes, "Obeah is a creole phenomenon, and it travels in diaspora."[38] She further highlights the writings of Charles Kingsley, a priest traveling throughout the Caribbean from the Church of England in the mid-nineteenth century, who notably emphasizes how natural materials may be infused with spirit or intention by an Obeah practitioner. "Thus, anything may become Obeah," according to Kingsley.[39] The flexibility of material components and creolization born of dislocation imbues Obeah with adaptability and transmutability in the face of forced displacement.

Obeah offers resources to the current desire for environmental ethics to address the ever-increasing movement of human populations away from the lands of their ancestry and birth. In this time of climate disruption, such realities are driven not only by economic opportunity without regard to environmental impact but also by environmental displacement and migration as the lived realities of climate disruption are experienced in everyday ways. Western environmentalism has romanticized the human connection to Earth and intimate knowledge of the land that comes from families rooting in place for a hundred years or more. Such values often stem from the writings of Aldo Leopold's call to understand ourselves as just one part of a greater land community. Yet there is an immediate and urgent need to find new ways to embed ourselves in the earth community through experiences of intensive— and even violent—separation from lands that we know.

In the early 1800s, when planter society was well established in Jamaica, enslaved communities had an inherited need for reconnection with new lands for their very survival. The use of provision grounds in plantation life meant that a sense of association and family in relationship to land had a direct impact on sustenance, health, and well-being in enslaved communities. There is documented use of Obeah practices to bind families to their provision grounds in clear violation of property law and economic standards in plantation life. These rituals, compounded by rituals connected to births, deaths, and land allegiances, offered a sense of place and community in the face of intense violation.[40] There is much to learn from the agency granted through such practices in material relation to the natural world.

Records of the traditions of Obeah credit customs that relied on the supernatural to catalyze change with multiple forms of resistance among communities of the African diaspora both pre- and post-emancipation. Common concerns pre-emancipation centered on the use of poison against enslavers, particularly by Black women.[41] Historian Sasha Turner Bryson argues that this emphasis results more from European understandings of poison as central to witchcraft than a true reflection of the practices of Obeah. The fear of poison often centered around enslaved Black women because of their intimate—though unwanted—proximity to planters when in domestic roles. Bryson argues convincingly that rather than minimizing the brutality of such women's experiences as somehow more privileged than those working in the fields, their inhumane realities of child death, sexual violence, ruthless exploitation, and unfeeling separation from the community must be acknowledged and respected. Such devastation logically inspires the acts of resistance and reclaimed agency that we see in the historical record when domestics are documented in legal cases as members of a highly orchestrated system of Obeah-as-resistance, sometimes by poisoning. Throughout the Caribbean, there are accusations against Black women lashing out against their enslavers and their enslavers' children as an attempt to free themselves from endless suffering.[42] There are suspicions of Black women in domestic roles serving as the center of larger-scale communal efforts to obliterate the plantocracy. Whether as individual practitioners or working in concert with others, Black women served as the focal point of an organized effort to undermine the daily devastations of plantation life.[43] Regardless of which role or motivation centered their actions, there is no question that Obeah offered agency in a situation designed to dehumanize. The practices of Obeah can be used for healing, they can be used for poisoning, they can be used for a reckoning and recompense against injustice, and they can be used for protection and an investment in personal and communal freedom. The choice over whether and how to make use of such methods—to be the hand of healing or the one that serves poison—allows for a level of resistance that rightly caused great distress among enslavers and colonial authorities alike.

While the wide-ranging practices of Obeah are not primarily focused on poisonings, a review of Jamaican legal proceedings emphasizes both poisoning and rebellion as primary fears among planters.[44] Often Obeah was credited with causing incurable diseases or securing an uprising's inexplicable success, where the material components of Obeah (usually drawn from Earth's body or the human body) were mixed into enslavers' food or clothing, or rubbed and carried on the bodies of the enslaved to imbue them with protection and strength.[45] The most famous of these was Tacky's Rebellion in Jamaica in 1760, where Tacky himself was described as an Obeah man whose oaths required of insurgents served to unify the community and hold them true to their purpose.[46]

Studies of slave rebellions frequently list Obeah as an empowering force and the source of great fear among white enslavers. Obeah oaths were common practice in preparation for revolt, where those committed to acts of insurgence promised their loyalty to one another and received protection and blessing for the uprising.[47] This created not only a sense of communal empowerment but also profound accountability. Spiritually and culturally it was unimaginable to betray an oath taken through the practices of Obeah.[48] The trepidation over potential repercussions was greater than the fear of the very real dangers associated with rebellion. The practices of Obeah wield strict consequences and demand careful respect, and as such can be utilized to prioritize balance and communal accountability. Communal accountability, for all that it can certainly be misused or misapplied, remains a badly needed tool in resisting environmental degradation. While the present-day realities of climate disruption also come with very real personal dangers, systems of shared valuation that can keep communal and personal behaviors immune from apathy and overwhelm remain a badly needed addition to environmental ethics writ large.

Tacky's Rebellion was so impactful that the very first anti-Obeah laws in Jamaica were passed the same year.[49] Tacky was both identified in the historical record as a "famous obeiah [*sic*] man or priest," and also said to rely on Obeah practitioners as his primary advisors.[50] The power of Obeah—whether as supernatural influence, communal accountability, reclamation of agency, or all three—led to a new understanding of the fragility of the plantocracy (or slavocracy) worldview. Tacky's Rebellion threatened not only the common acceptance of British colonialism and enslavement but also the very real lived realities of planters on the island. The uprising in April 1760 involved over one thousand enslaved individuals and resulted in the deaths of sixty white enslavers. An immense amount of property was destroyed during the rebellion, which by legal definition at the time included the more than five hundred enslaved people who were killed and later the additional five hundred who were exiled from Jamaica. There was an immense impact on planters and colonial authorities, both economically and in terms of their own sense of safety and authority.[51] The wave of legal interventions following Tacky's Rebellion speaks to this shift in their sense of security and well-being.

Remarkably, even though Tacky was executed and his decapitated head displayed by the roadside while other captured Obeah practitioners were burned at the stake and otherwise publicly tortured, the response of the enslaved community was continued rebellions.[52] Something in the force of binding oaths and protective workings allowed for the reclamation of agency and authority in entirely new ways. Public terrorism on the part of enslavers proved insufficient to dampen the strength of this uprising. Historian Vincent Brown writes of the time period immediately following Tacky's Rebellion as one where the struggle for spiritual authority became central to the maintenance of dominance and control by white enslavers. Even those who dismissed the power of Obeah to enact real change noticed its utility in driving enslaved communities to highly organized rebellion and political action.[53] Criminologist and anthropologist Mindie Lazarus-Black notes that in this Obeah functions, unsurprisingly, much like the law. It serves as a balancing system wielding both behavioral conscriptions and accountability. Through such balance came communal strength.

> Obeah was neither simple magic nor uncivilized religion. It was and remains an empowering phenomenon, a discourse and practice concerning rights, crime and

punishment, and varying forms of domination and resistance. Like law, obeah can generate violence or mitigate its consequences. Like law, it can "name," as one of my informants once put it, with far-reaching consequences for a person's reputation, status, and fate. Yet obeah contrasts sharply with law in its assumptions about the locus for authority and the nature of command. It does not locate power in the control of commodities or ownership of human labor. Obeah reorders social status, power, and hierarchy through its capacity to change people's characters, to compel or retrain action, to alter health, to claim possessions, or to fix a person's fate. To allow the full range of its capacity to influence the course of human affairs, obeah is best conceptualized as part of a wider system of illegalities that counters hegemony.[54]

In short, Obeah at its best functions like a system of moral principles grounded in the beliefs, traditions, and struggles of the broader community. It responds to a higher law, just like a religious ethic. Reclaiming the ethics of Obeah as a morally neutral drive toward balance (similar to the workings of a healthy ecosystem) allows us to see what has been categorized as Obeah from a different and renewed perspective, and provides important seeds for developing ecowomanist ethics.

As a creolized inheritance rooted in traditions from a range of African cultures, Obeah's utility as a morally neutral enterprise needs to be engaged through the religious and spiritual values of the source communities from which its practices emerged. Stewart's robust engagement of Jamaican religious experiences documents how the foundational source traditions of Obeah carry a characteristic moral neutrality. Outside of imposed European religious norms, African traditions frequently situate moral authority, accountability, and responsibility in relationship and through individual agency. Morality is neither prescribed nor predetermined, but impacted by condition and lived experience.[55] This inherited wisdom is fully expressed in womanist virtue ethics through the work of ethicist Katie Cannon and others. While Obeah's practices express a range of intentions for drawing on spiritual forces to make the change, their overarching impact within enslaved communities was to work toward an easing of collective suffering.[56] With its focus on capacity rather than good versus evil, an inherited African diasporic religious ethic has the situational integrity to utilize a range of healing, sustaining, and spiritual perspectives as well as a profound array of combative efforts to undermine and effectively annihilate systems set on community destruction.

Critical to Obeah in an ecowomanist frame is its potential to return agency in ways that do not rely on the dehumanization, domination, or control of others. Yet white enslavers obscenely worked to co-opt its influence for that precise purpose, even as they lacked an authentic ancestral connection to Obeah's creolized power. When Obeah is compromised by cultural thievery,

misappropriation, and control, it additionally illustrates its own utility for the
reclamation of dignity and agency. Vincent Brown's work in *The Reaper's
Garden* devastatingly depicts the power of even the suggestion that Obeah
practices might function in the hands of enslavers. This intentional wielding
of the imagery and intensity of practices white planters did not truly understand against the enslaved community was an effective terrorism strategy in
plantation life.

Brown focuses on death as a societally defining locus of power and control
in plantation life in Jamaica. His exploration of Obeah (and the more ritual-
ized Myal) centers on the engagement of spirits and fractured bodies as a
type of necromancy. At a time of such focused annihilation of Black bodies
to force mass production of agricultural goods from the Earth, alongside the
risk taking of white bodies differently and willfully exposed to increased risk
of death in the hope of financial gain in Jamaica, those who wielded death as
control had the power to shape plantation life.[57] For enslaved laborers, this
frequently meant work to disrupt the hegemony of white planters' control.
Yet the structures of castigation utilized both by planters and the courts
against the enslaved community appropriated the trappings of Obeah connected to the use of spirits or ghosts to curse and control. A good example
is the amputation as punishment.[58] The use of forcibly severed body parts
to desecrate sacred sites, such as particular types of trees or other natural
areas, adds an intentional level of mental defilement that is best understood
in relation to the agency Obeah would otherwise provide. By performative
mimicry—a literal blackface on the controlling structures of enslavement—
planters and colonial governmental structures appropriated the symbols and
beliefs of Obeah to disempower one of the few avenues of resistance against
enslaving and settler colonial norms.

The appropriation, mischaracterization, and vilification of Obeah regularly
exploited its embodied and material nature to define and control Black bodies. Colonial engagement with Black women's practices of Obeah increased
in years between British abolition of the slave trade and emancipation, as the
brutalization of their bodies came with greater financial consequences. From
an economic perspective, white enslavers suddenly had to control enslaved
women's reproductive labor with care for their survival, which called into
question any suspected source of agency and power. Rather than omitting
them from commentaries on Obeah as before, Obeah became a method by
which colonizers could continue to define Black women's embodiment for
their own benefit.[59] The legal record chronicles the shift in focus on Obeah
practices from Black men to women between the abolition of the British
slave trade and emancipation. Over a twenty-year period leading up to 1830,
Black women went from comprising just under 12 percent of those accused
of Obeah-related crimes in Jamaica to being perceived as the majority of

practitioners—older Black women in particular.[60] Once again the Black body served as a site of minimization and control, but even the power of colonial fictions and the white gaze were not enough to silence the agential norms authorized by these traditions.

Constructing an ecowomanist ethic requires resistance to the dominant canon of religious ethics that understands agency almost entirely from a ruling class, temporarily able-bodied, cisgender, white male perspective. As Cannon insists in her foundational work on Black women's moral wisdom,

> Blacks may use action guides that have never been considered within the scope of traditional codes of faithful living. Racism, gender discrimination, and economic exploitation, as inherited, age-long, complexes, require the black community to create and cultivate values and virtues in their own terms so that they prevail against the odds with moral integrity.[61]

European fears of the transmission of wisdom, agency, and community accountability through practices that came to be known as Obeah served to construct a long-standing imaginary where blatantly racist language and structures of control highlight a profound European—and later European ancestral—terror of losing dominance and legal ownership over colonized and enslaved communities. Yet the historical record catalogs the beneficial impact of Obeah on enslaved communities themselves, almost in spite of itself.[62] Where plantocracy and slavocracy offered terror and dehumanization, the practices that came to be known as Obeah offered dignity, agency, and accountability to and with Earth itself in relationship to the ancestors and all that was held as Holy in community. For ecowomanist work, this not only allows a return to the dignity that Beverly Mitchell identifies as the unassailable core of our humanity (see "A Humanity Worth Holding Onto"), but also offers a return to balanced and accountable relationality with Earth even in the face of the unimaginable. What could be more timely in the work of combating environmental devastation?

Obeah contains the possibility of reclaiming one's humanity before God by entering into ethical contracts through Earth as a conduit to both ancestry and a larger authority. It is true that some practices labeled as Obeah can be performed in the hope of controlling another or selfishly imposing one's own will on the world. Not all customs are altruistic or aim to create greater justice and healing. Yet there is balance in that many such practices are founded on ongoing spiritual and communal relationships and include a contract (of sorts) with the ancestors or spirits that would mitigate such actions, as would the knowledge that someone could retaliate through similar choices. Any power can be abused. What makes Obeah different in the reclamation of agency is that drawing on spiritual and Earth energy to exact change is held in a larger framework than simply the will of the practitioner or the Obeah woman the seeker has petitioned for help. We rarely manage to ascribe agency outside of the context of domination. An outside (human) entity always has the ability to grant agency or to take it away. In situations where the removal of agency is systematic and brutal in the extreme, having the ability to reclaim power on one's own terms (even as part of a larger and at times dangerous contract) matters. Being held accountable even within a reclaiming practice gives hope in times of environmental devastation.

Our humanity is strengthened when we draw lessons from life reclaimed in the midst of such devastation and suffering. Obeah—and, I argue, a variety of inherited environmental cultures and practices—allows us to center Earth's epistemology in badly needed ways. It invites us to know as our ancestors did that the land itself offers to us blueprints for survival, even when the land is relatively new to our knowing because of the lasting impact of forced displacement and harm. Still we might hold a handful of earth in ritual space, tuck within it an offering from our own bodies or an ancestor's earthly power—from a resident bird, predator, or blooming plant—simply to imbue that Earth with the wisdom of what is lived and therefore known. We are invited in turn to seek the strength or faithfulness to bind ourselves to the consequences of an ecosystem's knowing, literally a drive to balance and sustainability that might not include us in a final sustainable plan for earth community. Yet still that binding, that ethical contract, and that submission of self to the larger whole serve to return us to our inherent humanity.

Engaging the practices amalgamated and vilified via historic understandings of Obeah not only provides the right questions for an ecowomanist ethic, but it also surpasses the anthropocentric notion of "returning" some portion of agency to Earth and instead acknowledges Earth itself as a highly influential system with the capacity to hold humanity accountable. Such accountability, then, requires of us ethics centered on balance, aware of natural materials and nonhuman nature as a locus of moral authority, and inherently bound to the faithful commitments we make in relationship to all of creation. Ecowomanism, grounded in an embodied community ethic, provides us with new epistemological guidance to better understand our humanity in the face of climate disruption. Rather than reasserting a problematic human-centeredness that further distances our understanding of self from that same accountability, ecowomanism calls for a trauma-informed moral anthropology that cannot conceive of human nature as over against, or separate from, Earth itself. As survivors of the inconceivable, as carriers of cultural values and communal accountability, and as those who have never been allowed to reject or forget our own embodiment, women in the African diaspora have a unique understanding of how a moral refusal to compromise our humanity provides the very conditions needed to survive what was once an inconceivable level of environmental devastation. That wisdom redefines our understanding of survival itself, and in doing so gives us new knowledge on what it means to live a value-centered, human life.

A HUMANITY WORTH HOLDING ON TO

Historical theologian Beverly Mitchell argues that the dehumanization of those pushed to the margins and made low in society offers us a window into understanding the immutable aspects of human nature. She draws on the lived experiences of those who endured the Holocaust and chattel slavery to expose that which remains after "pride and pretense, illusions of grandeur, and notions of complete independence" are stripped away.[63] This she identifies as human dignity—most particularly, dignity in our suffering before God. Dignity becomes central to our understanding of theological anthropology because it is the unassailable core that endures when all else is stripped away through immoral and inhuman acts. This understanding of human nature does not valorize suffering but focuses instead on what is inextinguishable and of God. Dignity reminds us of our interrelatedness, and unites us as one species of our earth community where each member has a sacred connection to God.[64] Dignity also serves as a primary buffer to losing our humanity. It interrupts the unspeakable and strengthens the inviolable, sundering a willful apathy and resting our gaze on all that causes suffering and diminishment.[65]

In this analysis, it is dignity itself that serves as a corrective to the problem of dehumanization. Drawing on the work of philosopher Emmanuel Levinas, Mitchell coins the term "sins of defacement" to describe the violation of another's dignity. Dignity keeps us mindful of the sacrality of our human state, and averse to the violation of basic human rights that comes with the forcible reduction of another's humanity.[66] By definition, dignity should therefore also increase our mindfulness of the sacrality of all creation, as it is through our interrelatedness that we are reminded of the central meaning of our own nature. In theological terms, respect for the dignity of all expressions of life not only calls us to recognize the goodness and the glory of God reflected in all humanity, it further disallows indifference as a response to both human degradation and environmental devastation. Dignity identifies the profound hubris inherent to such acts. It is only with this knowledge at the forefront of our understanding of what it means to be human that we can fully explore what it means to be human in relation to all of creation.

To dignity and defacement we must add sins of defilement if we are to place questions of human nature in dialogue with environmental devastation. Womanist theologian Delores Williams writes of sins of defilement as coexisting affronts to the inherent sacrality of both Black women and Earth.

Attributing entitled indifference and a presumed blamelessness as the same forces silencing the abuse of the planet and of once-enslaved Black women's bodies for the sake of white Americans' physical comfort and ease, Williams insists that sins of defilement are centered on the desacralization of creation rather than the more traditional understanding of sin as a betrayal of our commitments before God. These shared violations center on a denial of the possibility of true consciousness or intellect in Black woman and Earth, and a demonizing of anything caricaturized as primal or dark.[67] "This defilement of nature's body and of black women's bodies is sin, since its occurrence denies that black women and nature are made in the image of God," writes Williams. "Its occurrence is an assault upon the spirit of creation in women and nature."[68] Societal justifications further sanitize those who benefit from such desecration by normalizing their privilege, such that dominant cultures never have to bear witness to the consequences of such atrocities and often spend years debating the veracity of related claims. The removal of agency through exploitation and abuse frequently seeks to force those so violated to divorce themselves from an understanding of their own goodness. This undermines attempts at liberation and invites an inevitable future destruction that arrives seemingly by surprise and with great lamentation but requires none who brought it into being to bear responsibility for their actions.

Instead we are made more fully human by defining our humanity in environmental terms, rejecting the anthropocentrism that values a small fraction of humanity over all nonhuman nature. Too often liberationists seeking to dismantle various forms of oppression have affirmed the inherent value of all humanity without first interrogating their foundational concept of the human person itself. Even radical critiques of Enlightenment thinking have not moved beyond long-standing narratives of human exceptionalism. The notions of superiority that sustain environmentally destructive behaviors, upheld by hypotheses casting humans as both unique and superior to nature, are also central to the justification of dehumanizing behaviors that threaten the dignity of those most marginalized throughout human history. Ecofeminist Anna Peterson, one of few scholars linking questions of environmental sustainability with ideas of human nature, recommends interrupting this worldview through the work of ethical anthropology in order to explicitly connect our ontology with our values. To do so she calls us to resist seeking one single universalized understanding of human beings and instead draw on cross-cultural understandings to engage a broader truth.[69]

Peterson is explicitly seeking ethical understandings that have the capacity to permanently change behavior, casting environmental ethics as lived ethics whose moral principles directly impact how human groups manage the decisions of daily life. The goal is to center narratives with the capacity for shifting dominant worldviews, such as the establishment of an enduring human/nature dualism dating back to foundational tenets of Western philosophy. Here the trope of human exceptionalism gains particular strength from Christian theological anthropology through the *imago dei* (which is frequently tied to dominion over nonhuman nature) and the teaching that only humans have a rational soul.[70] These teachings are brutally effective for sanitizing the immorality that is central to sustaining the violence against Black women and Earth that Williams defines as sins of defilement. Peterson is particularly interested in religious narratives that create a group sense of identity by shaping our relationships, claiming that religious ethics gain their power from being embedded in stories. It is vital that we learn how such stories guide our behavioral practices in order to best draw on religious teachings for environmental engagement.[71]

To explore this question the work of ethical anthropology turns to social constructivism, where human nature is understood as developed to completion through particular cultural constructs that are specific to a given time and place. Peterson is careful to challenge the tendency in social constructivism to devalue embodiment (since human development is furthered by cultural, rather than physical elements) that in turn lessens the value of nature, a tendency that links back to Christian theological anthropology as well.[72] She seeks to recast social constructivism by placing it into dialogue with multiple religious worldviews, doing this in the hopes of gleaning knowledge about the world that is located in its various cultures rather than promoting cross-cultural dialogue simply for the sake of diversity.[73] Peterson is intentional about speaking to the inherent complexities of comparative ethics yet also argues for the benefit of engaging multiple worldviews for undermining false universalist tendencies in preparation for reconstructing our ideologies.[74]

While the need for a cross-cultural methodology is convincing, Peterson falters in her approach by privileging the voices of white scholars and practitioners in religious traditions outside of their own cultural groups. She also fails to engage the live issue of forced displacement, whether by violence or migration resulting from climate change, which both interrupts and troubles the development of human nature in ways specific to time and place. Ecowomanism, placed in dialogue with questions raised by ethical anthropology in an environmental frame, not only offers the engagement of underutilized narratives but also further centers humanity that can be understood *across* the lived realities of time and place without devolving to a false universality. As a decolonizing, diasporic, multireligious environmental ethic, ecowomansim neatly shifts worldviews through the seemingly obvious practice of theorizing from a completely different foundation.

Defilement and defacement resolve in the lived histories of Black bodies broken for the idolatry of a maximized agricultural productivity without care for human or Earth's labor or well-being. Black bodies and Earth's systems are reimagined and disparaged as fragmented modes of existence, where neither is assigned agency nor understood as worthy of care because we have long forgotten to value what is broken, even by our own sins. This is not to say that stereotypical depictions of brokenness, particularly in relationship to human disability, can be labeled (libeled) as resulting from prior sinfulness. Rather, the sacred wholeness and purposefulness of all creation must not be diminished either through a stereotyping of that which is embodied in diverse ways or through a supposed erasure of inherent value through human violence and violation.

The fragmentation of human bodies and Earth is richly documented as a site of theorizing human personhood through the work of literary scholar Monique Allewaert. Allewaert writes of a creolized ontology born in the American plantations of the eighteenth century, where enslaved peoples were defined as something less than human. This evolving "parahuman" status, enforced through the type of violation that is both a sin of defacement and a sin of defilement, nonetheless encouraged a knowing of self in relation to a broader creation. The forced displacement of diverse African peoples brought together under duress not only created creolized cultures but further created newly emergent ways of knowing the self that were influenced not only by human diversity but also through engagement with new earth communities as well.[75] These reconstructed ways of knowing returned personhood to those whose dignity, as understood by Beverly Mitchell, was under threat. Even in the face of the unimaginable, creolized ontologies sustained agency and enhanced the likelihood of survival.

In direct contradiction to the dehumanization that saturated chattel slavery and plantation life, the embrace of fractured bodies (what Allewaert describes as bodies reduced to parts) and nonhuman nature offered a new category of being. While enslavers and colonial authorities understood this category of parahuman to be inherently ruined and less than human, Allewaert posits the categories of human, parahuman, and animal as parallel and of equal worth in the traditional hierarchies that categorize the value of all life.[76] This understanding of the parahuman builds on similar acts of terrorism to those identified by Vincent Brown in Jamaican plantation life. Africans' bodies were reduced to parts through the violence of plantation life and similar forms of amputation as punishment, and fragmentation became central to the understanding of the self.[77] Here the intention was to justify the definition of enslaved peoples as less than human, rather than to performatively co-opt their magical practices as a form of control. Yet the practices of Obeah relate to both scholars' theories.

Allewaert describes Obeah as one of many "botanico-religious ontologies" that associate human and nonhuman animals as an evolving interrelated mode of being, at the material level, that identify reclaimable power and agency in the points of connection between human and nonhuman life.[78] While parahumanity for Allewaert remains an important—and equal in value to humanity—understanding of personhood, I would argue that a creolized ontology that situates humanity (no matter how violated) in relation to the natural world is in fact a restorative understanding that promotes the reclamation not only of our full humanity but also of an interrelatedness to all creation that has integrity at its core. Allewaert's work insists that this lived experience creates a new category of personhood that disallows a simple return to understanding ourselves as human.[79]

I argue that intentionally reclaiming our ontologies born in the face of unimaginable suffering invites us to an ecowomanist moral anthropology that rejects the possibility of understanding human nature as separate from our relatedness to the rest of creation. This relatedness cannot be defined in terms of superiority, stewardship, ownership, or any other ideology predicated on the defilement of nonhuman nature, but instead must center on an inherent, accountable connection that refutes any understanding of humanity as separated from, or placed above, the broader earth community. Freed of inherited Enlightenment definitions of how to be faithfully human in our living, we are liberated to reclaim an intrinsic interrelatedness that sustains our dignity even in the midst of the suffering that is already born of climate devastation.

The lived experience of Black women teaches us that agency is not an indispensable part of our humanity, though its violation is dehumanizing. We have learned this nuance through generations of disenfranchisement. Dignity, as Mitchell reminds us, is inherent to our humanity. No amount of disempowerment can undermine our intrinsic worth before God. While this subtle difference is minimized in dominant (and especially domineering) cultures, we can identify its impact through the immense efforts taken to convince marginalized groups that they are worthless and to convince members of dominant cultures that other groups of individuals are not fully human. The primary function of internalized oppression is to manipulate marginalized peoples so that they attack their own sense of dignity and therefore undermine the strength that comes from an unassailable human worth. Agency relies on a temporal power that is buoyed by systems and institutions that define our rights and abilities to choose for ourselves. Dignity, with its moral center outside of our agential opportunities, can be denied but never erased.

We know that our dignity is stronger than the forces of suffering because of our mothers who "made do." In environmental terms, separating a community from its own power as amplified and held accountable by Earth can only serve as a method of control so long as the central lie of disconnection is maintained. At stake in the reclamation of inherited environmental cultures is a return to dignity—both as a force of liberation rooted in earth justice and as a reinvestment in our very humanity. Ecowomanism as a decolonizing, diasporic, multireligious environmental ethic becomes not only a liberating force but also a site of repair through the reclamation of transgenerational knowledge. Earth epistemologies root us in our knowing and free us to retain our humanity in the name of our justice-centered faiths, even in the face of unimaginable climate disruption.

An ecowomanist ethic unflinchingly denounces the desecration of Earth through the forced labors of defiled and defaced human bodies, no matter their race, gender, religion, or cultural heritage. An ecowomanist ethic reclaims beauty and wholeness, most particularly within the lived experiences and transmitted wisdoms of those whose dignity has been tested (though never erased) by all who would hide their sins in the open wounds of those they have violated, including Earth. An ecowomanist ethic retrieves the unassailable dignity at the center of our lived existence and knows that by our own grace we can choose to offer hard-won transgenerational knowledge to the very sites and peoples that have harmed us, for the salvation of Earth and all creation. An ecowomanist ethic will not sacrifice our humanity in the face of environmental devastation. Our dignity before God serves as a guide and shield before all that would tempt us to exchange our humanity for the paltry and ultimately false protection of a brief delay in experiencing the onset of suffering that already plagues those whose threatened dignity we choose to ignore.

Justice can stop a curse by recentering our human living on that which promotes balance and restores wholeness to all of creation.

NOTES

1. For a robust exploration of master narratives in environmental philosophy see Plumwood, *Feminism and the Mastery of Nature*.

2. A term coined by ecologist Eugene Stormer and chemist Paul Crutzen to denote the current geological age when human beings have had a defining impact on Earth's ecosystems.

3. Beverly Eileen Mitchell, *Plantations and Death Camps: Religion, Ideology, and Human Dignity* (Minneapolis: Fortress Press, 2009), 44–47.

4. Delores Williams, "Sin, Nature, and Black Women's Bodies," in *Ecofeminism and the Sacred*, ed. Carol J. Adams (New York: Continuum, 1993), 24–25.

5. Monique Allewaert, *Ariel's Ecology: Plantations, Personhood, and Colonialism in the American Tropics* (Minneapolis: University of Minnesota Press, 2013), 2.

6. Anna L. Peterson, *Being Human: Ethics, Environment, and Our Place in the World* (Berkeley: University of California Press, 2001), 185.

7. As stated in chapter 1, this chapter does not depict or list exhaustive examples of the specific practices of Obeah. Such anthropological cataloging is both outside the scope of this project and also intentionally omitted in order to honor the intellectual

property and agency of Obeah's practitioners. I am not an expert in such practices outside of those I have inherited from my own family and ancestral lines. For a cataloging of one culture's expression of current practices, see Dianne M. Stewart, *Three Eyes for the Journey: African Dimensions of the Jamaican Religious Experience* (New York: Oxford University Press, 2005) and Claudette A. Anderson, "Gnostic *Obia* from *Chukwu Abiama* to Jah Rastafari: A Theology of the JamAfrican Obia Catholic Church" (PhD diss., Emory University, 2010).

8. Willis Jenkins, *The Future of Ethics: Sustainability, Social Justice, and Religious Creativity* (Washington, DC: Georgetown University Press, 2013), 1.

9. Jenkins, *Future of Ethics*, 17.

10. Olive Senior, *Working Miracles: Women's Lives in the English-Speaking Caribbean* (Bloomington: Indiana University Press, 1991), 129–30.

11. Karen Baker-Fletcher, *A Singing Something: Womanist Reflections on Anna Julia Cooper* (New York: Crossroad, 1994), 195–98.

12. See Monica Coleman, *Making a Way out of No Way: A Womanist Theology* (Minneapolis: Fortress Press, 2008).

13. Jenkins, *The Future of Ethics*, 11.

14. Jenkins, *The Future of Ethics*, 128.

15. Mayra Rivera, *The Touch of Transcendence: A Postcolonial Theology of God* (Louisville: Westminster John Knox Press, 2007).

16. Rivera, *Touch of Transcendence*, 41–47, 64–65, 69–75.

17. Walker, *Our Mothers' Gardens,* preface.

18. Walker, *Our Mothers' Gardens,* 339–40.

19. Walker, *Our Mothers' Gardens,* 338–39.

20. Jeffrey Cottrell, "At the End of the Trade: Obeah and Black Women in the Colonial Imaginary," *Atlantic Studies* 12, no. 2 (2015): 202–03.

21. Horace Mills, "Jamaica Moving to Legalize Obeah, a Practice Banned for Centuries," *Jamaica Beacon*, June 5, 2019, https://jamaicabeacon.com/news/jamaica-moving-to-legalize-obeah-a-practice-banned-for-centuries.

22. Kenneth M. Bilby and Jerome S. Handler, "Obeah: Healing and Protection in West Indian Slave Life," *Journal of Caribbean History* 38, no. 2 (2004): 156, 162.

23. Bilby and Handler, "Obeah," 157.

24. Joseph Williams, *Voodoos and Obeahs: Phases of West India Witchcraft* (1932; repr., San Bernadino, CA: Simplicissimus Book Farm, 2016), 210–12.

25. Williams, *Voodoos and Obeahs*, 216–17.

26. Williams, *Voodoos and Obeahs*, 214, 228–29.

27. Stewart, *Three Eyes for the Journey*, 43, 177.

28. Albert E. Bell, "Jingles," *Panama American*, May 7, 1926, 510–11.

29. Lara Putnam, "Rites of Power and Rumors of Race: The Circulation of Supernatural Knowledge in the Caribbean, 1890–1940," in *Obeah and Other Powers: The Politics of Caribbean Religion and Healing,* ed. Diana Paton and Maarit Forde (Durham, NC: Duke University Press, 2012), 243.

30. Lauren Derby, "Sorcery in the Black Atlantic: The Occult Arts in Comparative Perspective," *Journal of Interdisciplinary History* 44, no. 2 (Autumn 2013): 236, https://doi.org/10.1162/JINH_a_00538.

31. Anderson, "Gnostic *Obia*," 183, 199.

32. Jerome S. Handler and Kenneth M. Bilby, "On the Early Use and Origin of the Term 'Obeah' in Barbados and the Anglophone Caribbean," *Slavery and Abolition* 22, no. 2 (2001): 87, https://doi.org/10.1080/714005192.

33. Handler and Bilby, "Early Use and Origin of the Term 'Obeah,'" 88–89.

34. Stewart, *Three Eyes for the Journey*, 42.

35. Bilby and Handler, "Obeah," 163–65.

36. Sasha Turner Bryson, "The Art of Power: Poison and Obeah Accusations and the Struggle for Dominance and Survival in Jamaica's Slave Society," *Caribbean Studies* 41, no. 2 (July–December 2013): 73, https://doi.org/10.1353/crb.2013.0030.

37. Williams, *Voodoos and Obeahs*, 259.

38. Aisha Khan, "Dark Arts and Diaspora," *Diaspora* 17, no. 1 (2008): 52.

39. Khan, "Dark Arts and Diaspora," 52.

40. Bryson, "The Art of Power," 76.

41. Bryson, "The Art of Power," 63, 69–70.

42. Bryson, "The Art of Power," 69–70.

43. Bryson, "The Art of Power," 69–70.

44. Bryson, "The Art of Power," 63–64.

45. Margarite Fernández Olmos and Lizabeth Paravisini-Gebert, *Creole Religions of the Caribbean: An Introduction from Vodou and Santería to Obeah and Espiritismo*, 2nd ed. (New York: New York University Press, 2011), 156–58.

46. Bryson, "The Art of Power," 63.

47. Stewart, *Three Eyes for the Journey*, 42–43; Khan, "Dark Arts and Diaspora," 57–58.

48. Anderson, "Gnostic *Obia*," 67.

49. Bryson, "The Art of Power," 64.

50. Bryson, "The Art of Power," 63; Vincent Brown, *The Reaper's Garden: Death and Power in the World of Atlantic Slavery* (Cambridge, MA: Harvard University Press, 2008), 149.

51. Brown, *Reaper's Garden*, 148–49.

52. Brown, *Reaper's Garden*, 148–49.

53. Brown, *Reaper's Garden*, 144–45, 149–50.

54. Mindie Lazarus-Black, *Legitimate Acts and Illegal Encounters: Law and Society in Antigua and Barbuda* (Washington, DC: Smithsonian Institution Press, 1994), 54.

55. Stewart, *Three Eyes for the Journey*, 62–64, 183.

56. Bilby and Handler, "Obeah," 155.

57. Brown, *Reaper's Garden*, 4–5, 12.

58. Brown, *Reaper's Garden*, 142–43, 150.

59. Cottrell, "At the End of the Trade," 200–2, 208.

60. Vincent Brown, "Spiritual Terror and Sacred Authority in Jamaican Slave Society," *Slavery and Abolition* 24, no. 1 (2003): 39, https://doi.org/10.1080/714005263.

61. Cannon, *Katie's Cannon*, 58.

62. Bilby and Handler, "Obeah," 158–60.

63. Mitchell, *Plantations and Death Camps*, 40.

64. Mitchell, *Plantations and Death Camps*, 40.

65. Mitchell, *Plantations and Death Camps*, 47–50.

66. Mitchell, *Plantations and Death Camps*, 50–53.

67. Williams, "Black Women's Bodies," 24–25, 27–28.

68. Williams, "Black Women's Bodies," 29.

69. Peterson, *Being Human*, 1–3, 39–42.

70. Peterson, *Being Human*, 4, 20, 28–30.

71. Peterson, *Being Human*, 17, 22.

72. Peterson, *Being Human*, 53–54, 60–61.

73. Peterson, *Being Human*, 69–70.

74. Peterson, *Being Human*, 78–79.

75. Allewaert, *Ariel's Ecology*, 6–7.

76. Allewaert, *Ariel's Ecology*, 86.

77. Allewaert, *Ariel's Ecology*, 85, 104.

78. Allewaert, *Ariel's Ecology*, 7, 9–11.

79. Allewaert, *Ariel's Ecology*, 86–87.

Conclusion

My belief in both the utility and urgency of emerging ecowomanist responses to environmental devastation has only grown over the course of this project. I am convinced that there is no one singular ethical solution to the realities of our time. For decades, womanist scholars have insisted that false universals in the study of theology and ethics serve to dehumanize and silence the most vulnerable among us. This remains true in womanist engagements with both Earth-honoring faiths and the need to restore our relationships to Earth itself. There are no shortcuts in the work of environmental ethics, and the ideologies that entice us to believe in one simplistic truth that applies to all of creation too often become the very principles that instigate violence in an already hurting world. Instead it is time for an intercultural morality.

We need transnational approaches, ones that demand close examination of the overlapping, interconnected realities of the sites of climate disruption. Our analyses must be conducted in environmental time, over long enough periods to allow Earth itself to have a voice. We need not only generations of Earth knowledge but also polyphonic literacies of the current moment, with its ecosystems balance and inherited environmental cultures, even across displacements writ large. New ways of knowing must engage the broadest range of factors as we struggle to understand what is needful and necessary. We require diasporic approaches, multireligious methodologies, transgenerational narratives, and decolonial tools to reclaim and unpack the inherited environmental cultures silenced in service of imperialist white supremacist capitalist heteropatriarchy. We also must have sustaining traditions across the rich and glorious expressions of spiritual truths to revitalize our own knowing as we strive to simply "make do."

For generations, our mothers labored to make do in the service of our survival—the survival of our families, our communities, our traditions, and our sense of well-being. Most of our mothers are still making do. We need their same strength to ascribe value and embrace making do as more than enough, hopefully helping us to dismantle the insatiable desire to overconsume. And we have an obligation to extend their teachings to a much broader portion of the human family, particularly to those of us in the Global North who know little more than the desire to possess everything and everyone. Here is where our faith communities most need to divest themselves of toxic ideologies while at the same time lending their salvific strength to the enterprise. We must not let the language of faith decompose in the hands of those who would wield it solely to justify a few more rounds of insatiable greed before Earth has no more to give. I am reminded that moral neutrality, as discussed in the teachings drawn from Obeah, is in line with the balance of nature. Ecowomanist ethics must not seek to replicate the eschatological goals of individual religious traditions, no matter how meaningful, but must instead center the balance required for life's thriving in an Earthly history. Let there be no telos that valorizes the quickening of an afterlife for the very planet.

There will be many who read this invitation to recenter our moral covenant with creation in inherited environmental knowledge as a refusal to clearly outline the steps required to save humanity and the planet. Here is the deeper invitation, one that requires hard work and tenacity to instead let go of our assumptions that either the latest innovation will save us without any need for sacrifice or societal reconstruction, or that we can make a lasting change based on what we already know. It is in the rejection of foundational supremacist tropes of domination that casually seek to enslave both peoples of the global majority and Earth itself that the beginnings of another path might be found. But it requires unflinching vigilance to continually reject the sanitizing justifications of rapacious settler colonial logics masquerading as markers of success in a capitalist society driven by cannibalistic ideologies of progress. Let us name the untenable and immoral consumption of the so-called developed nations honestly. For it is by eating those regularly pushed to the margins and that which would otherwise sustain life that we "succeeded" in creating such imbalance across the planet.

As an individual, I am neither free from nor absolved of this complicity. And recent studies show clearly that a small number of companies in the fossil fuel industry are responsible for the majority of human-driven climate devastation since the start of the Anthropocene.[1] As many have stated before me, focusing the language of faith solely on individual behavior is but one more distraction from the overarching ideologies driving irreparable destruction. The stories that we tell in environmental time must challenge the very foundations of how we societally face the consequences of environmental harm. Recent events have illustrated this need to a calamitous degree.

Editing this project in the time of Covid-19 means the historical reduction of West Indian communities to "reservoir(s) of infected people" at the time of canal construction is never far from my mind. US government officials in the early 1900s fighting the spread of malaria only in areas housing white employees while vilifying Black laborers as vectors of disease is as ruinously ignorant as the Trump administration spreading misinformation and refusing to create a comprehensive plan to fight the spread of the novel coronavirus once its heightened impact on Black and brown communities became clear. It is as catastrophically self-destructive as prioritizing vaccines for countries that cause and temporarily benefit from the majority of environmental harm while leaving others around the globe unresourced in the fight against this pandemic. Both malaria and Covid-19 carry indicators of environmental devastation. Both diseases require a comprehensive response. The same ideologies used to sanitize the impact of colonialism and racialized violence across generations are used to ignore the obvious need to prevent the spread of disease in all peoples whether or not one celebrates the full sacrality of Black and brown bodies. The same ideologies used to ignore, mismanage, and racialize the impact of these diseases resulted in needless deaths due to malaria and needless deaths due to Covid-19.

Climate denial is intimately interwoven with racist ideologies. The progression of such logics consistently follows well-worn grooves that are anti-science, anti-environment, founded in white supremacy culture, and used to foment the lie that settler colonial capitalism can be used to promote the common good. Not even the need for self-preservation proves strong enough to intervene. Imposed fictions of immorality have become the habitual justification for defilement and covenant rupture with Earth. This lies at the root of climate devastation today. We need new ways of knowing, free of the distractions and deceptions that annihilate that which makes us most human within Earth's community. It is past time for us to be accountable to Earth's own wisdom.

New understandings of self, formed in response to our relation to Earth, are vital to a faithful slowing of environmental devastation. These should be informed by dialogue with climate and environmental sciences so that together we might find a greater ability to put knowledge into sustainable practice. Without a nuanced understanding of the decimating legacies of colonialism and neo-imperialism, we operate with only a partial knowledge of the systems that sustain devastation. A refusal to engage the full reality of climate disruption guarantees the continuation of injustice even from within our efforts to make change. To that end, I believe we need much greater study of the US Department of Agriculture, specifically the environmental impacts of its policies, history, and ideologies in lands both within and outside the United States. It is past time to reject narratives that pardon US neo-imperialism as somehow less malevolent than European colonial rule.

I am heartened by the stories of women in the African diaspora who live(d) with a faithful strength that surpasses my own imagination. It is their witness—whether through survival, teaching, organizing, healing, preserving family, or creating art—that reminds me of a grace that transcends my own understanding. I tell the students whom I am privileged to teach that hope is a spiritual discipline. It is not a panacea, nor is it a litmus test for our readiness to serve as religious leaders or scholars in hard times. It is instead a magnetic north, a point of reorientation that might serve as a corrective when the collective weight of toxic ideologies and faithless decisions in the wider world would keep us from our own best knowing. May we sacrifice enough to retain the full significance of our humanity in the face of climate disaster. May we together, with humility and lamentation, work to ease collective suffering.

In the end, I honor the souls of all peoples and all beings resting with the Canal itself. I honor the life that trickled through a hole in the dike drop by drop at first—"little trinkles of water"—like old thickened tears cried between the generations, distilled through the fire of our striving to form balm for those currently enfleshed. I see myself here, in the salve for the very violence that can never be greater than our collective strength. "My soul has grown deep like the rivers." Langston Hughes knew. A rushing / running / grounding / LIVELY movement of strength woven clear and new from the sinew and the longing and the perseverance of all who came before. Water is life. Is life. Is life. Is life life (l)*ife*.

May we learn by making do.

NOTE

1. For a comprehensive analysis of how fossil fuel producers are responsible for producing the vast majority of greenhouse gas emissions, see Richard Heede, "Tracing anthropogenic carbon dioxide and methane emissions to fossil fuel and cement producers, 1854-2010," *Climatic Change* 122 (2014): 229–241, DOI 10.1007/ s10584-013-0986-y.

Bibliography

Allewaert, Monique. *Ariel's Ecology: Plantations, Personhood, and Colonialism in the American Tropics*. Minneapolis: University of Minnesota Press, 2013.

Anderson, Claudette A. "Gnostic *Obia* from *Chukwu Abiama* to Jah Rastafari: A Theology of the JamAfrican Obia Catholic Church." PhD diss., Emory University, 2010.

Annual Reports of the Canal Zone Experiment Gardens for the Fiscal Years 1935 and 1936. Mount Hope, Canal Zone: Panama Canal Press, 1939.

Arp, William, III, and Keith Boeckelman. "Religiosity: A Source of Black Environmentalism and Empowerment?" *Journal of Black Studies* 28, no. 2 (November 1997): 255–67.

Baker-Fletcher, Karen. *A Singing Something: Womanist Reflections on Anna Julia Cooper*. New York: Crossroad, 1994.

Baker-Fletcher, Karen. *Sisters of Dust, Sisters of Spirit: Womanist Wordings on God and Creation*. Minneapolis: Augsburg Press, 1998.

Bauman, Whitney. *Theology, Creation, and Environmental Ethics: From Creatio Ex Nihilo to Terra Nullius*. New York: Routledge, 2009.

Bedford, Nancy Elizabeth. "Making Spaces: Latin American and Latina Feminist Theologies on the Cusp of Interculturality." In *Feminist Intercultural Theology: Latina Explorations for a Just World*, edited by María Pilar Aquino and Maria José Rosado-Nunes. New York: Orbis Books, 2007.

Bell, Albert E. "Jingles." *Panama American*, May 7, 1926.

Bennett, Hugh H., and Wm. A. Taylor. *The Agricultural Possibilities of the Canal Zone*, parts 1–2, prepared for the US Department of Agriculture, Office of the Secretary, Bureau of Soils and Bureau of Plant Industry. Washington, DC: Government Printing Office, 1912. https://ufdc.ufl.edu/AA00029633/00001.

Betancourt, Sofía. "Between Dishwater and the River: Toward an Ecowomanist Methodology." In *Ecowomanism, Religion, and Ecology*, edited by Melanie Harris. Leiden: Brill, 2017.

Bigelow, Poultney. "Our Mismanagement at Panama." *Independent*, January 4, 1906. Reprinted in *Message from the President of the United States Transmitting Certain Papers to Accompany His Message of January 8, 1906*, 79–91. Washington, DC: Government Publishing Office, 1906.

Bilby, Kenneth M., and Jerome S. Handler. "Obeah: Healing and Protection in West Indian Slave Life." *Journal of Caribbean History* 38, no. 2 (2004): 153–83.

Brooks, Mark. "Economic Growth, Ecological Limits, and the Proposed Expansion of the Panama Canal." Master's thesis, McGill University, 2005.

Brown, Vincent. *The Reaper's Garden: Death and Power in the World of Atlantic Slavery*. Cambridge, MA: Harvard University Press, 2008.

Bryson, Sasha Turner. "The Art of Power: Poison and Obeah Accusations and the Struggle for Dominance and Survival in Jamaica's Slave Society." *Caribbean Studies* 41, no. 2 (July–December 2013): 61–90. https://doi.org/10.1353/crb.2013.0030.

Bullard, Robert. "Environmental Justice in the Twenty-First Century." In *The Quest for Environmental Justice: Human Rights and the Politics of Pollution*, edited by Robert Bullard, 19–42. San Francisco: Sierra Club Books, 2005.

Campbell, Ronica (pseudonym). Interview by Alison Saunders, June 30, 2011. MP3 video, 19:29.

Campusano, María Cristina Ventura. "Between Oppression and Resistance: From the Capture of the Imaginary to the Journey of the Intercultural." In *Feminist Intercultural Theology: Latina Explorations for a Just World*, edited by María Pilar Aquino and María José Rosado-Nunes, 179–195. New York: Orbis Books, 2007.

Cannon, Katie G. *Black Womanist Ethics*. Atlanta: Scholars Press, 1988.

———. *Katie's Canon: Womanism and the Soul of the Black Community*. New York: Continuum International, 2008.

Caro, Olga Consuelo Vélez. "Toward a Feminist Intercultural Theology." In *Feminist Intercultural Theology: Latina Explorations for a Just World*, edited by María Pilar Aquino and Maria José Rosado-Nunes, 248–264. New York: Orbis Books, 2007.

Carse, Ashley. *Beyond the Big Ditch: Politics, Ecology, and Infrastructure at the Panama Canal*. Cambridge, MA: MIT Press, 2014.

———. "Nature as Infrastructure: Making and Managing the Panama Canal Watershed." *Social Studies of Science* 42, no. 4 (2012): 539–63. https://doi.org/10.1177/0306312712440166.

Cheng, Chu-Chueh. "Frances Trollope's America and Anna Leonowen's Siam." In *Gender, Genre, and Identity in Women's Travel Writing*, edited by Kristi Siegel, 123–166. New York: Peter Lang, 2004.

Coleman, Monica. *Making a Way Out of No Way: A Womanist Theology*. Minneapolis: Fortress Press, 2008.

Core, Sue, and Ann Cordts McKeown. *Isthmiana*. Panama City: Panama American Publishing Company, 1939.

Cornish, Vaughan. "The Panama Canal in 1908." *Geographical Journal* 33, no. 2 (February 1909): 153–77.

Cottrell, Jeffrey. "At the End of the Trade: Obeah and Black Women in the Colonial Imaginary." *Atlantic Studies* 12, no. 2 (2015): 200–18.

Curtin, Deane. *Environmental Ethics for a Postcolonial World.* Lanham, MD: Rowman & Littlefield, 2005.

Davis, Irie (pseudonym). Interview by Alison Saunders, June 30, 2011. MP3 video, 10:59.

de Goodin, Melva Lowe. *People of African Ancestry in Panama 1501–2012.* Panamá City: Imprenta Sibauste, 2014.

Derby, Lauren. "Sorcery in the Black Atlantic: The Occult Arts in Comparative Perspective." *Journal of Interdisciplinary History* 44, no. 2 (Autumn 2013): 235–44. https://doi.org/10.1162/JINH_a_00538.

"Destruction of Last Dike," *Canal Record,* October 15, 1913.

Douglas, Kelly Brown. *Sexuality and the Black Church.* New York: Orbis Books, 1999.

Farajajé, Ibrahim. "Organic Multireligiosity and Seriously (Warning: Coloured) Organic Scholarship." Facebook, August 26, 2012. https://www.facebook.com /notes/khalvat-dar-anjuman/organic-multireligiosity-and-seriously-warning -coloured-organic-scholarship/10151226711691579/.

Fitzmaurice, Andrew. "The Genealogy of *Terra Nullius.*" *Australian Historical Studies* 38, no. 129 (2007): 1–15. https://doi.org/10.1080/10314610708601228.

Flores-Villalobos, Joan. "'Freak Letters': Tracing Gender, Race, and Diaspora in the Panama Canal Archive." *Small Axe* 23, no. 2 (July 2019): 34–56. https://doi.org/10 .1215/07990537-7703266.

Frederick, Rhonda D. *"Colón Man a Come": Mythographies of Panamá Canal Migration.* Lanham, MD: Lexington Books, 2005.

Frenkel, Stephen. "Geographical Representations of the 'Other': The Landscape of the Panama Canal Zone." *Journal of Historical Geography* 28, no. 1 (2002): 85–99. https://doi.org/10.1006/jhge.2001.0375.

———. "Geography, Empire, and Environmental Determinism." *Geographical Review* 82, no. 2 (April 1992): 143–53. https://doi.org/10.2307/215428.

———. "Jungle Stories: North American Representations of Tropical Panama." *Geographical Review* 86, no. 3(July 1996): 317–33.

Grant, Jacquelyn. "Tasks of a Prophetic Church." In *Theology in the Americas: Detroit II Conference Papers,* edited by Cornel West, Caridad Guidote, and Margaret Coakley, 136–42. Maryknoll, NY: Orbis Books, 1982.

Grant, Kady (pseudonym). Interview by Alison Saunders, June 30, 2011. MP3 video, 11:51.

Greenberg, Amy S. *Manifest Manhood and the Antebellum American Empire.* Cambridge: Cambridge University Press, 2005.

Greene, Julie. *The Canal Builders: Making America's Empire at the Panama Canal.* New York: Penguin Books, 2009.

Halstead, Murat. *Pictorial History of America's New Possessions: The Isthmian Canals and the Problem of Expansion.* Chicago: W. S. Reeve, 1899.

Handler, Jerome S., and Kenneth M. Bilby. "On the Early Use and Origin of the Term 'Obeah' in Barbados and the Anglophone Caribbean." *Slavery and Abolition* 22, no. 2 (2001): 87–100. https://doi.org/10.1080/714005192.

Harris, Melanie L. *Ecowomanism: African American Women and Earth-Honoring Faiths.* New York: Orbis Books, 2017.

Heede, Richard. "Tracing anthropogenic carbon dioxide and methane emissions to fossil fuel and cement producers, 1854-2010." *Climatic Change* 122 (2014): 229–41. https://doi.org/10.1007/s10584-013-0986-y.

Hendricks, Thomas. "Race and Desire in the Porno-Tropics: Ethnographic Perspectives from the Post-colony." *Sexualities* 17, nos. 1–2 (2014): 213–29. https://doi.org/10.1177/1363460713511100.

Investigation of Panama Canal Matters: Hearings before the Committee on Oceanic Canals of the United States Senate in the Matter of the Senate Resolution Adopted January 9, 1906, Providing for an Investigation of Matters Relating to the Panama Canal, Etc., vols. 1–4 (Washington, DC: Government Printing Office, 1907).

Isasi-Díaz, Ada María. *Mujerista Theology: A Theology for the Twenty-First Century.* New York: Orbis Books, 2002.

Jenkins, Ruth Y. "The Gaze of the Victorian Woman Traveler." In *Gender, Genre, and Identity in Women's Travel Writing*, edited by Kristi Siegel, 15–30. New York: Peter Lang, 2004.

Jenkins, Willis. *The Future of Ethics: Sustainability, Social Justice, and Religious Creativity.* Washington, DC: Georgetown University Press, 2013.

Johnson, Cassandra. "A Consideration of Collective Memory in African American Attachment to Wildland Recreation Places." *Human Ecology Review* 5, no. 1 (1998): 5–15. https://www.jstor.org/stable/24707101.

Khan, Aisha. "Dark Arts and Diaspora." *Diaspora* 17, no. 1 (2008): 40–63.

Kelley, Joyce E. *Excursions into Modernism: Women Writers, Travel, and the Body.* Burlington, VT: Ashgate, 2015.

LeFeber, Walter. *The Panama Canal: The Crisis in Historical Perspective.* New York: Oxford University Press, 1978.

Lazarus-Black, Mindie. *Legitimate Acts and Illegal Encounters: Law and Society in Antigua and Barbuda.* Washington, DC: Smithsonian Institution Press, 1994.

Leopold, Aldo. *A Sand County Almanac: With Essays on Conservation from Round River.* New York: Ballantine Books, 1966.

Maparyan, Layli. *The Womanist Idea.* New York: Routledge, 2012.

McClintock, Anne. *Imperial Leather: Race, Gender, and Sexuality in the Colonial Context.* New York: Routledge, 1995.

McCullough, David. *The Path between the Seas: The Creation of the Panama Canal 1870–1914.* New York: Simon & Schuster, 1977.

McGroarty, John, M. H. Walsh, and J. K. Baxter. *Macwalbax: A Collection of Poems, Cartoons, and Comment.* Panama City: The Panama Times, 1926.

McKittrick, Katherine. *Demonic Grounds: Black Women and the Cartographies of Struggle.* Minneapolis: University of Minnesota Press, 2006.

Mills, Horace. "Jamaica Moving to Legalize Obeah, a Practice Banned for Centuries." *Jamaica Beacon*, June 5, 2019. https://jamaicabeacon.com/news/jamaica-moving-to-legalize-obeah-a-practice-banned-for-centuries.

Mitchell, Beverly Eileen. *Plantations and Death Camps: Religion, Ideology, and Human Dignity.* Minneapolis: Fortress Press, 2009.

Moreno, Stanley Hackerdom. "Impact of Development on the Panama Canal Environment." In "The Future of Panama and the Canal," edited by Richard L.

Millett, special issue, *Journal of Interamerican Studies and World Affairs* 35, no. 3 (Autumn, 1993): 129–49. https://doi.org/10.2307/165971.

Newton, Velma. *The Silver Men: West Indian Labour Migration to Panama 1850–1914.* Kingston: Ian Randle, 2004.

Nixon, Rob. *Slow Violence and the Environmentalism of the Poor.* Boston: Harvard University Press, 2011.

Olmos, Margarite Fernández, and Lizabeth Paravisini-Gebert. *Creole Religions of the Caribbean: An Introduction from Vodou and Santería to Obeah and Espiritismo,* 2nd ed. New York: New York University Press, 2011.

O'Reggio, Trevor. *Between Alienation and Citizenship: The Evolution of Black West Indian Society in Panama 1914–1964.* Lanham, MD: University Press of America, 2006.

Osei-Tutu, Kwaku. "Growth of the Atlantic Slave Trade: Racial Slavery in the New World." In *Color Struck: Essays on Race and Ethnicity in Global Perspective,* edited by Julius O. Adekunle and Hettie V. Williams, 93–112. Lanham, MD: University Press of America, 2012.

"'Panama Dreams' – A documentary by Alison Saunders." Interview by TTT Live Online, September 19, 2019. Video, 6:35. https://www.youtube.com/watch?v =pUUSi0Dytx0.

Parker, Elizabeth Kittredge. *Panama Canal Bride: A Story of Construction Days.* New York: Exposition Press, 1955.

Parker, Matthew. *Panama Fever: The Epic Story of One of the Greatest Human Achievements of All Time—The Building of the Panama Canal.* New York: Doubleday, 2007.

Peterson, Anna L. *Being Human: Ethics, Environment, and Our Place in the World.* Berkeley: University of California Press, 2001.

Plumwood, Val. *Environmental Culture: The Ecological Crisis of Reason.* London: Routledge, 2002.

———. *Feminism and the Mastery of Nature.* London: Routledge, 1993.

Price, Archibald Grenfell. *White Settlers in the Tropics.* New York: American Geographical Society, 1939.

Putnam, Lara. "Eventually Alien: The Multigenerational Saga of West Indians in Central America 1870–1940." In *Blacks & Blackness in Central America: Between Race and Place,* edited by Lowell Gudmundson and Justin Wolfe, 278–306. Durham, NC: Duke University Press, 2010.

———. "Rites of Power and Rumors of Race: The Circulation of Supernatural Knowledge in the Caribbean, 1890–1940." In *Obeah and Other Powers: The Politics of Caribbean Religion and Healing,* edited by Diana Paton and Maarit Forde, 243–67. Durham, NC: Duke University Press, 2012.

Reyes Rivas, Eyra Marcela. *El trabajo de las mujeres en la historia de la Construcción del Canal de Panamá 1881–1914.* Panamá City: Universidad de Panamá Insituto de la Mujer, 2000.

Riley, Shamara Shantu. "Ecology Is a Sistah's Issue Too: The Politics of Emergent Afrocentric Ecowomanism." In *This Sacred Earth: Religion, Nature, Environment,* 2nd ed., edited by Roger Gottlieb, 412–27. New York: Routledge, 2004.

Rivera, Mayra. *The Touch of Transcendence: A Postcolonial Theology of God.* Louisville: Westminster John Knox Press, 2007.

Rodríguez, Jeanette. "Tripuenteando: Journey toward Identity, the Academy, and Solidarity." In *Feminist Intercultural Theology: Latina Explorations for a Just World*, edited by María Pilar Aquino and Maria José Rosado-Nunes, 70–88. New York: Orbis Books, 2007.

Rounsevell, Nelson. *The Life Story of N.R., or 40 Years of Rambling, Gambling and Publishing.* Panama City: Panama American Publishing Co., 1933.

Senior, Olive. *Dying to Better Themselves: West Indians and the Building of the Panama Canal.* Kingston: University of the West Indies Press, 2014.

———. *Gardening in the Tropics.* Toronto: Insomniac Press, 2005.

———. *Working Miracles: Women's Lives in the English-Speaking Caribbean.* Bloomington: Indiana University Press, 1991.

Smith, Christina. "Saunders Makes History with 'Panama Dreams.'" *Loop Barbados*, March 23, 2018. http://www.loopnewsbarbados.com/content/saunders-makes-history-panama-dreams.

Smith, David M. *Moral Geographies: Ethics in a World of Difference.* Edinburgh: Edinburgh University Press, 2000.

Stewart, Dianne M. *Three Eyes for the Journey: African Dimensions of the Jamaican Religious Experience.* New York: Oxford University Press, 2005.

Sutter, Paul S. "Nature's Agents or Agents of Empire? Entomological Workers and Environmental Change during the Construction of the Panama Canal." *Isis* 98, no. 4 (December 2007): 724–54. https://doi.org/10.1086/529265.

Thompson, Krista A. *An Eye for the Tropics: Tourism, Photography, and Framing the Caribbean Picturesque.* Durham, NC: Duke University Press, 2006.

Townes, Emilie. *In a Blaze of Glory: Womanist Spirituality as Social Witness.* Nashville: Abingdon Press, 1995.

———. *Womanist Ethics and the Cultural Production of Evil.* New York: Palgrave Macmillan, 2006.

Tribble, Phillis. *Texts of Terror: Literary-Feminist Readings of Biblical Narrative.* Philadelphia: Fortress Press, 1984.

Van Alstyne, Richard W. "The Panama Canal: A Classical Case of an Imperial Hangover." *Journal of Contemporary History* 15, no. 2 (April 1980): 299–316. https://doi.org/10.1177/002200948001500205.

Vargas-Betancourt, Margarita. "Finding the Silver Voice: Afro-Antilleans in the Panama Canal Museum Collection at the University of Florida." Paper presented at the 13th International Conference on Caribbean Literature, "Panama in the Caribbean: The Caribbean in Panama." University of Panama, Panama City, November 13–16, 2013.

Walker, Alice. *In Search of Our Mother's Gardens: Womanist Prose.* San Diego: Harcourt Brace Jovanovich, 1983.

Weekes, Melanie, and Kimberly Bourne. "Cooking Bajan Style: Breadfruit Cou-Cou." *The Blog, Loop Barbados*, January 8, 2014, https://loopbarbados.com/loop-blog/cooking-bajan-style-breadfruit-cou-cou.

Welch, Sharon D. *A Feminist Ethic of Risk*, rev. ed. Minneapolis: Fortress Press, 2000.

Westerman, George. "Fifty Years of West Indian Life on the Isthmus of Panama." Unpublished manuscript, typescript. George Westerman Collection (MG505 101/1), Schomburg Center for Research in Black Culture, New York Public Library.

White, Lynn, Jr. "The Historical Roots of our Ecologic Crisis." *Science* 155, no. 3767 (March 10, 1967): 1203–7. https://doi.org/10.1126/science.155.3767.1203.

Williams, Delores. "Sin, Nature, and Black Women's Bodies." In *Ecofeminism and the Sacred*, edited by Carol J. Adams, 24–29. New York: Continuum, 1993.

———. *Sisters in the Wilderness: The Challenge of Womanist God-Talk*. New York: Orbis Books, 1993.

Williams, Joseph. *Voodoos and Obeahs: Phases of West India Witchcraft*. 1932. Reprint, San Bernadino, CA: Simplicissimus Book Farm, 2016.

Appendix A

Employment and Marital Status of Martinique Women on the Isthmus of Panamá, January 1906

Name	Marital Status (Years)	Job
Rose Mont Rose		"Was sweeping camp quarters and now I am washing as I can make more money."
Ezio Eliza	married (6)	"I came to join my husband, who is working in the bake shop."
Evelina Sovos		"Since I came I have been steady at work."
Denne Catherine	single	"I am employed at the hotel here and am furnished quarters."
Alexandria Bartillo	married (12)	"My husband is a carpenter and I help by doing housework. I have two children."
Visione Laveray	single	"I am now working in the residence of one of the chiefs here, making general work, washing, etc."
Pauline Gertrude		"I am working now doing washing and ironing."
Familia Johnbaptist	married (5)	"I came here to join my husband, who came before me, and am now living with him at Paraiso."
Cornelia Brazan	single	"I am now working as house servant for a family in Paraiso."
Violin Feroline	married (3)	"He is working in the canal. I attend to our house."
Alfonsin Alfonse	married (1)	"I do our housework. He supports me."
Louane Stevens	single	"I wash and iron for anyone . . . making about $12 a month."
Maselle Present	single	"Am employed at the commissary and well satisfied. I am not living an immoral life."
Vision Alexander		"My health has not been good since I came. Other-wise I am doing well whenever I am well enough."

(Continued)

Name	Marital Status (Years)	Job
Cameillia Jarbin	single	"I have had plenty of work at the canteen."
Janie Torrent	married	"[Came] here . . . following my husband, who is a laborer here. I help him by washing and ironing for other people."
Louisa Lorent	married	"My husband paid my passage. He is a carpenter here and I keep house for him. I have no children."
Rose Pelagi		"Since coming here I have done well washing and ironing."
Mercedes Clarie	married (2)	"My husband is a carpenter working for the Canal Commission. I . . . came here to join him."
Cecil Daily	married (7)	"My husband is a carpenter working for the Interoceanic Canal Commission."
Marie Robin	single	"I am living at Paraiso, and am employed as a laundress in the hotel here."
Lorena Joucent	single	"I have a very good place and work as a domestic in Paraiso."
Decani Julia	married (5)	"He is a laborer on the canal and I live with him here."
Denis Alexia	married (7)	"I have been sick and unable to work. I am married to Mr. Blony. . . . He is a laborer on the canal."
Pauline St. Paul	single	"I am a house servant here for a foreman in the shops. . . . I am not married, but do not live an immoral life."
Camille Staniclas	married	"Came here to my husband, who is a workman on the railroad. . . . I help along by washing and ironing."
Almaide Charles	single	"I am at work at the hotel since I have been here . . . and am well treated there and get good wages."
Dennis Denir	single	"I had work until I hurt my hand and under the care of a doctor."
Maria Bouman	single	"Have been doing general washing ever since I came."
Angela Fanoi	single	"I am now washing for various people for a living."
Estafan Lendo	single	"I am now washing for various parties."
Leoni John	single	"I am now working as laundress at the Paraiso Hotel."
Vanalia Ovia	single	"I am now washing and ironing for various people."
Policia Maria	single	"I am now working about as washerwoman from place to place."
Henrietta Irrinese	single	"I am now washing and ironing for various people."

Name	Marital Status (Years)	Job
Maria Julia	single	"I paid my fare here. I am a domestic in the family of Mr. Taylor. I sleep, eat, and am paid good wages there."
Averline Crospeh	single	"I am now working as a laundress . . . have been a little sick. I do not live an immoral life."
Lucie Luber	single	"I do washing and ironing for anybody."
Rose Blaise		"Ever since I came I am working here at the hotel and earning a good living."
Josephine Benzon	single	"My brother is here working on the canal as a laborer. I live with him and work doing washing and ironing."
Francilia St. Rose	married (3)	"I came here to join my husband who . . . [is] employed as a laborer on the canal."
Louise Baya	married (5)	"I am working at the Cantina. Have not been well part of the time."
Eugenie Dumas	single	"I am working since I came as a washwoman."
Ferdilia Capron	single	"My trade is making cigars. . . . I do any work that comes handy."
Louisa Saville	single	"Since I came I have got work, washing and ironing."
Ida Raymond	single	"I am acquainted with two other girls here from Martinique . . . who are working in American families."
Janie Louisa		"The family seem to love me when I am working. I do nursing for the baby of the family."
Ononia Johns		"I am working in an American family . . . and I like the man, wife, and children."
Cecil Fanton		"I came and got work with good wages."
Matra Arvet	single	"Ever since I came I have been employed at the hotel and get good wages."
Nelson Bellmore	single	"I am now house servant for an American family in Corosal."
Jane Gremore	single	"Since I came I got work at the hotel as a servant. . . . I get $8 a month with board."
Cedona Daniels	single	"I am now employed as a laundress at the hotel here."
Lucy Dafarti	single	"Am now employed as washerwoman at the Interoceanic Canal Commission Hotel in Corosal."
Lionel Balison	single	"I am working at the hotel steady since I came. We all eat there and get good food and wages."
Samdoul Sawf	married (3)	"I am employed at the hotel washing and other housework. My husband . . . works in sanitary department."
Zanda Oska	married	"My husband and son are both assisting as carpenters and I am washing, with my daughter, for other laborers."

(Continued)

Name	Marital Status (Years)	Job
Louise Maxmion	single	"I am employed at the chief carpenter's house, doing washing, cooking, and general housework."
Ella Lee Antwerp	single	"I am now employed as a laundress at the Isthmian Canal Commision hotel at Corozal."
Gabrielle Blauze	single	"I am employed to wash at the hotel."
Leonie St. Rose	single	"I am now employed as a domestic in the house of the postmaster at Corosal."
Maria Louise Missett	married	"I am not working now, having been in hospital. My husband keeps me so I don't have to work hard."
Clement Calestine	single	"I now work as a domestic at the hotel in Corosal."
Lucie Jermay		"I have been employed at the hotel here as a laundress."
Francoise Alpfonse		"Since I came here I have been working at the hotel."
Ida Raymond	single	"I am now washing for a living."
Maria Berti	married (2)	"I have had work ever since I came, as a servant. I work with Mr. Campbell at the commissary."
Lucille Cuffy	single	"I get about $20 a month as a domestic, doing general housework."
Metillia Modest	married (1)	"I am a domestic. . . . My husband is a laborer on the work here."
Naomy Etiene	married (4)	"My husband is a laborer and we both make good wages, as I wash and iron."
Julia Waugram	married (1)	"I am now living with my husband at Rio Grane [sic] . . . and work, doing washing, etc. to help out."
Marie Elino	married (3)	"I have been working as a laundress . . . with my husband who is a laborer on the canal at Rio Grande."
Normia Lucia	single	"Have been working as a laundress ever since I arrived."
Eubena Barise	married (1)	"I work for Mr. Sablo as a domestic. . . . [My husband] works at Empire for the Canal Commission."
Alexandria Piquot	married (1)	"I have not found all the work I could do. . . . My husband came here before me, and I came to him."
Ophelia Horton	single	"I am engaged in washing and ironing. I am doing fairly well."
Antonio Dennis	married (3)	"My husband came before I did, and I came to him. I work out as a servant to help him along."
Julia Alfred	married (5)	"I am married and came here to join my husband, who came before me."

Name	Marital Status (Years)	Job
Francuise Laulow	single	"I am now working with the family of Joseph Gastan as a domestic. I live and sleep in the same house."
Alfonce Ustach	single	"I am working as a washerwoman at the hotel. . . . I am 69 years old. The morals of all the women in camp are good."
Urena J. Louis	single	"I have found work and am well paid."
Theodose Marmele	single	"I am now working at the hotel here."
Hermance Suvena	single	"I am working here at the hotel."
Adeline Balance	single	"I am working as a servant at hotel here."
Justine Papie	single	"I am working now at the hotel."
Anselle Louissie	single	"I work at the hotel here."
Louise Marrie	single	"I work as chambermaid at the hotel."
Amant Casteel	single	"Have been at work here at the hotel."
Therese Colete	single	"I have been at work here at the hotel and get fair wages."
Madlen Marie	married (1)	"My husband . . . is a laborer on the canal, and I live with him at Rio Grande."
Atinice Nosie	married (6)	"My husband came here before me, and I came to join. I am living with him now at Culebra, Canal Zone."
Leonie Janepiere	single	"I am now working for an American family in Culebra, Canal Zone, as a domestic servant."
Acelia Barray	single	"I am now working as a chambermaid at the hotel in Culebra, Canal Zone."
Adrienne J. Louis	single	"I am now working in the hotel at Culebra, Canal Zone, as chambermaid."
L. Jane Louis	single	"Am now working as chambermaid at the hotel in Culebra, Canal Zone."
Marie Vulnon	single	"I am now working as chambermaid in the hotel at Culebra, Canal Zone."
Margarete P. Pole	single	"I am now working as chambermaid at the hotel in Culebra."
Albertine Vadley	single	"I am now working as chambermaid in the hotel at Culebra."
Victoria Jane Joseph	married (1)	"I came to join [my husband], who works as a carpenter in building department in Cunette, Canal Zone."
Damshale Alphred	married (7)	"Came here with my husband, who works on the canal. I live with him in Cunette, Canal Zone."
Matile Elouice	married (1)	"Came here with my husband, who works in Culebra . . . in the track department. I live with my husband."
Louis Ponalaie	married (16)	"Came here with my husband, who works on the canal, but is now sick in the hospital. I live with him."

(Continued)

Name	Marital Status (Years)	Job
Ellen Vadlay	married (8)	"Came here with my husband, who works in track department on the canal. I live with him."
Pauline Marie Francie	married (1)	"I came with my husband, who works as a shoemaker in Empire, Canal Zone."
Bluempia Messon		"I am not working now, as I have fever. Before I was taken sick I worked as laundress in a hotel in Empire."
Buenett Kenegon	married (6)	"I came with my husband, who is now working in track department for the canal. I live with him at Cunette."
Catherine Maxemen	married (2)	"Came here with my husband, who is now working in the track department. . . . I live with him at Cunette, Canal Zone."
Jueilana Carmalin	married (1)	"My husband is working as a blacksmith in the machine shop. . . . I live with him at Cunette, Canal Zone."
Marcia Lando		"I am now working as kitchen servant at the hotel. . . . When I first arrived I was sick with fever."
Seraphine Fesan	married (5)	"My husband came first and I came later to join him, and am now living with him at Cunette, Canal Zone."
Jillui Richha	married (4)	"He works on the canal as a laborer. Jane Ortancia came on the same ship, and lives with my husband and myself."
Jane Ortancia	single	"My friend's husband came on the same boat with us and I came to live with them and work on the Zone."
Juilcia Auguistine	single	"I am now working as a washerwoman at Cunette, Canal Zone."
Obertine Noremie	single	"I work at the hotel in Empire. . . . At first I washed clothes, but now am employed at the hotel."
Jane Pratrice	married (1)	"[Was] informed I could come here and join my husband and get plenty of work. . . . He is employed in the track department."
Jane Alfonce	single	"I am now working as a washerwoman. . . . I do not live with a man or anyone else. . . . I work every day."
Louise Paulin	married (2)	"My husband came here to work, and I came later to join him. . . . He is a laborer on the canal."
Louise Leismoha	single	"I am working here in the Empire Hotel as helper in the kitchen."
Pheons Anie Romohnan	married	"I came with my husband. . . . He is a laborer, and I do washing and ironing."
Katherine Ernest	married	"I am now working as a laundress."

Name	Marital Status (Years)	Job
Lucianne Lucien	married (3)	"I am now living with my husband in Empire and doing odd work, such as washing, ironing, etc., to help him along."
Vuss Marie	married	"I am washing and ironing, and my husband is a laborer."
Hermine Paulain	single	"I now work as a washerwoman."
Denise Silma	single	"I now work as washerwoman and live alone by myself."
Toolida St. Louis	single	"I am now working as a washerwoman and earn my living this way. I live with another single Martinique woman."
Pauline Fage	married (3)	"Came here with my husband and now live with him at Gorgona, Canal Zone."
Amie Safargue	single	"I am now working as cook for Mr. Dumanoir and family."
Sedonie Labessiere	single	"I am now working as cook and laundress in the family of Charles Murdock at Gorgona, Canal Zone."
Irene Nica	married (2)	"I came to join my husband, who came before. I am now living with my husband in Gorgona, Canal Zone."
Edualice Chantelle	married (3)	"Came here to join my husband, who came before me. He works on the canal, and I live with him at Gorgona."
Bernadotte Eleanor	married (1)	"Came here to join my husband, who came before me. He works on the canal, and I live with him at Gorgona."
Constnace [sic] Nimaise	married (3)	"Came here to join my husband, who is working on the canal. I live with him at Gorgona, Canal Zone."
Finez Willy	married (1)	"I am now working as cook in a restaurant, and live in said restaurant."
Clotilde Simon	married (1)	"Came here to join my husband, who came before me. He works on the canal, and I live with him at Bas Matachin."
Louise Figaro	married (2)	"Came here to join my husband, who came before me. I am now living with him at Gorgona, Canal Zone."
Luce Nordeau	single	"I am now working as a washerwoman."
Satoute Miller	married (1)	"I came with my husband and live with him. . . . He now works as a laborer on the canal."
Antoinette Laonise	married (7)	"My husband works on the canal and I do washing."
Clement Gerald	married (1)	"He works as a painter, and I do domestic work in the family of Mr. Davis, and live with my husband."

(Continued)

Name	Marital Status (Years)	Job
Jani Senaie	married (4)	"He works on the Canal, and I take in washing. We live together at Bas Obispo."
Mary Angeline	married (9)	"He works on the canal, and I work as a domestic in the house of the doctor at Bas Obispo."
Suserine Johnbaptist	married (1)	"I came here with my husband, who works on the canal, and I take in washing."
Philomen Philibert	married (1)	"Came here with my husband, who works on the canal. I live with him at Bas Obispo and work as a laundress."
Felici Brillo	married (4)	"He works on the canal at Bas Obispo, and I live with him and work out as a laundress to help him out."
Luslee Lainte	married (6)	"My husband works on the canal. . . . I work as a domestic in an American family to help him."
Maria Josephine	married (7)	"I came here with my husband about two and one-half months ago. He works on the canal, and I live with him."
Geraldine Francis	married (1)	"He is working on the canal at Bas Obispo, and I am also working."
Taoiny Alois	married (4)	"My husband came here as a laborer two months before me. . . . He is a foreman at Bas Obispo, and we live together."
Gabriel Paralo	married (3)	"My husband works on the canal and I live with him."
Celia Ambroisine	married (1)	"I came here with my husband . . . working on the canal as a laborer. I am a domestic in the family of Mr. Davis."
Mirala Naomi	married (1)	"I came here with my husband . . . working on the canal as a laborer. . . . I help him by washing."
Mrs. Leona Louis	widowed	"I came here as a house servant in an American family."
Mrs. Dane Barclay	married (5)	"My husband is a foreman on canal work. I help him by doing washing."
Melanie Primeaux	single	"Since I have been here I have been sweeping the camps and keeping them clean. I work continuously."
Alcina Alcide	single	"Since arriving here have been employed in an American family as house servant."

Source: All data in this table are drawn from affidavits published in Investigation of Panama Canal Matters: Hearings before the United States Senate Committee on Interoceanic Canals [. . .], vols. 1–4 (Washington, DC: Government Printing Office, 1907), 941–81. Author.

Appendix B

Macwalbax *Excerpts*

"CARNIVAL DAYS IN PANAMA"[1]

Again the gladsome season comes,
    When Carnival is queen;
When all the carping cares of life
    Are banished from the scene;

When high and low and rich and poor
    In festive mood unite,
To honor gay Frivolity,
    With unconcealed delight.

The irksome tasks of every day
    We cheerfully forget;
About life's duties, stern and gray,
    We cease to fume and fret;

And round the common, work'day world,
    A golden web we weave;
For one brief while, we strut and smile,
    In the land of "Make Believe."

There's ample time in days to come,
    For dull, prosaic work;
But in the golden present hour,
    Such vexing thoughts we shirk;

O'er many a dull "mañana,"
    Grim Duty spreads her thrall,
But today's the day for pleasure.
    And we heed her sprightly call.

The common laborer displays
    An interest as keen,
As does the wealthy merchant prince,
    Complacent and serene;

And the humble washerwoman,
    In her simple honest heart
Is happily convinced that she
    Performs a vital part.
The tiny girl of tender years,
    Elaborately dressed,
In bright regalia now appears
    As eager as the rest;

The ancient dame with faded eyes,
    Tenaciously has clung,
To age-old custom, though she sighs
    For times when she was young.

The matron, sober and sedate,
    The maid of youthful bloom,
Alike, now don, in showy state,
    The Carnival costume;

The ancient streets of Panama
    With brilliant colors glow,
In fancy finery bedecked,
    A brave and blithesome show.

There's none so needy, none so poor,
    And none so dull of wit,
But in this frolicsome allure,
    He claims his modest bit;

And who'd begrudge the brief surcease,
    From sordid daily grind,
The welcome respite and relief
    For body and for mind?

From every corner of the earth,
    From every distant land
Imbued with merriment and mirth,
    At Folly's high command,

Are denizens of every race,
    In motley garb arrayed,
Each proud to claim a pompous place,
    In the Carnival parade.

Full soon will come the somber Lent,
    The penitential days,
When all, in solemn reverence bent,
    Must mend their worldly ways;

Ah, sí; we think about this thing
    In intermittent leisure;
Por qué? Our hearts still vagrant sing,
    The siren song of pleasure.

Today, we have not time nor taste,
    For trouble, toil or sorrow;
Religion, rigid, pure and chaste,
    We must embrace tomorrow;

But today, light thoughts inspire us,
    And Folly reigns serene,
So All Hail! the lovely Aida,
    For the nonce, our royal Queen.

"PANAMA'S MARKET PLACE"[2]

No doubt you've seen "Old Panama"—its ruins gaunt and hoary;
And ready with sympathetic heart its grim and tragic story;
No doubt you've viewed the old "Flat Arch"—A marvel in its may
And the gorgeous "Golden Altar" in the church of San Jose.

But let these old time relics, for the moment, lie in state,
And note with human interest the city up-to-date;
Observe the teeming multitudes of every type and race,
Who trade and traffic, buy and sell, in this old market place.

Down where the ancient city wall o'erlooks the sparkling bay,
A thousand dancing water craft aproach [sic] the busy quay,
Each brings its tiny cargo and though primitive and rude,
They carry freight of wealth untold—They bring the city's food.

Hard by this antique landing place the city market stands
With its rows of bustling merchants from many distant lands,
Like one gigantic beehive where gather, day by day,
The motley crowd of purchasers in chattering array.

The keen and crafty Chino is seen on every hand,
Methodical as clock work, efficient, cool and bland,
He listens with complacence to the housewife's shrill tirade,
He's utterly abused—but gets the biggest trade.

The silent, swart East Indian is eloquent in spells
As he extols the value of the merchandise he sells;
The ebony Jamaican, in adjective expert,
The native panamanian, intensive and alert.

The negro woman, Junoesque, proceeds with stately tread,
A basket full of merchandise upon her kinky head;
Her generous rotundity fills up the narrow aisle,
Disarming all resentment by her broad and potent smile.

The proud and pompous citizen with wealth at his command,
Whose purchases are carried by a servant near at hand;
The lean and "pobre" widow, who can barely find the price
Of two repulsive fish heads and a tiny bag of rice.

The ordinary "hombre" from somewhere down the coast
Whose marketable produce is trivial at most,
Astride his small "caballo" with a basket on each side,
In one of which is proudly borne his manhood's joy and pride.

His tiny daughter, eight years old, with eyes of velvet brown,
Who never has beheld till now the wonders of the town;
Alas, her father's scanty means are sorely stretched to meet
The cost of shoes and stockings for her bare and dainty feet.

So wags the weary world along, so grind the ruthless mills
Of Fate that knows not sympathy, with human hopes nor ills;
In Panama's old market place where crude and vivid souls
Depict the Human Comedy in all it's [*sic*] varied roles.

"THE WASH LADY"[3]

No Nordic blonde, with bright blue eyes,
That hold the tints of summer skies,
And golden hair and dainty size,
      Is Daisy;
My heroine is not that kind;
On sentimental stuff, I find,
Her practical, prosaic mind
      Is hazy;

No soulful yearnings has she got;
"Soft stuff" to her, is only rot;
But one thing, certainly, she's not—
      That's lazy.
I've often wondered how it came
That so inadequate a name
Was tacked upon the robust frame
      Of my wash lady.

They might have named her Jane or Chloe,
Jemima, Cicely or Flo,
Belinda, Abigail or Zoe,
      Or even Sadie;
But, in her frail and helpless youth,

Some joker, with a taste uncouth,
Must dub her "Daisy," though, in truth,
　　　　She's rather shady.

"A rose, by any other name,
Would smell as sweet," and look the same,
And Daisy seeks immortal fame
　　　　By washing clothes;
This strenuous and dusky queen
With her physique, would scorn to lean,
For help, upon a wash machine;
　　　　That's not her pose.
She has the strength to tear and rend
My wardrobe, scant, from end to end,
But small indeed, her power to mend—
　　　　She seldom sews.

Her apparatus is but rude;
Her working methods, quaintly crude,
But, with her energy imbued,
　　　　It's simple as you please;
A bar of soap and an ample tub,
A deft and perfunctory rub,
A slam or two with a hefty club—
　　　　The job is done with ease;

The clothes are dried upon the weeds,
(My comfort she so lightly heeds)
And that's why cockle burs and seeds
　　　　Adorn my B.V.D's.
But, Daisy, finding fault is vain;
If you'll forgive my speech, profane,
From future growls, I will refrain,
　　　　Although, you're queer;

Into this odd and cruel world,
We're all promiscuously hurled,
Without a guiding sign unfurled,
　　　　Our path to clear;
But, in life's plan, for good or ill,
A most important place you fill;
With all your faults, I love you still,
　　　　Oh Daisy dear.

"THE BANANA LADY"[4]

Oh you quaint Banana Lady, with the turban and the smile,
  And the tray of toothsome merchandise, in appetizing pile,
First glimpse of "local color," for the tourist's eager gaze,
  And picturesque example of the lure of tropic ways.

Oh the succulent banana is a delicacy rare
  And the fresh and fragrant mango is a treat beyond compare,
To the soldiers and the sailors and the militant marines,
  And the travelers from distant ports, who land 'mid tropic scenes.

Your homely, pleasant features are a vision of delight;
  Your patient, pensive attitude is restful to the sight;
Your black and beaming countenance, impassive and serene,
  Would grace a Moorish Princess, or an Abyssinian Queen.

Famed Cleopatra, in her barge, upon the classic Nile,
  Had no more regal stateliness, no more bewitching guile,
Than you can defly [*sic*] bring to bear, when, artfully betimes,
  You separate the public from their nickles and their dimes.

But, in your idle moments, whence that dignity, profound,
    So mystic and inscrutable, that girds you round and round?
Do you perhaps inherit that inimitable poise
    From some dead Nubian chieftain, past human griefs and joys?

Behind those somber, brooding eyes, that dark and stolid face,
    Persists the ancient tragedy and sorrow of your race;
But in your wise philosophy, there dwells no vengeful hate,
    As you sell your ripe bananas, smilling [*sic*] cheerily at Fate.

Oh for the calm serenity that marks thy simple soul;
    Oh for thy heart, contented, that accepts a humble role;
Oh for thy cheerful spirit that makes any life worth while;
    Oh thou quaint Banana Lady, with the turban and the smile.

NOTES

1. John McGroarty, M. H. Walsh, and J. K. Baxter, *Macwalbax: A Collection of Poems, Cartoons, and Comment* (Panama City: The Panama Times, 1926), 122–23.
2. McGroarty, Walsh, and Baxter, *Macwalbax*, 110.
3. McGroarty, Walsh, and Baxter, *Macwalbax*, 46–47.
4. McGroarty, Walsh, and Baxter, *Macwalbax*, 48.

Index

About the Author

Rev. **Dr. Sofía Betancourt** serves as associate dean for Academic Affairs at Drew University's Theological School. She holds a PhD in religious ethics and African American Studies from Yale University. Her academic work focuses on environmental ethics of liberation in a womanist and Latina feminist frame. She served for four years as the director of Racial and Ethnic Concerns of the Unitarian Universalist Association, and briefly as its interim co-president. Betancourt's ministry centers on work that is empowering and counter-oppressive. Betancourt holds a BS from Cornell University with a concentration in ethnobotany, an MA and MPhil from Yale University in religious ethics and African American studies, and an MDiv from Starr King School for the Ministry.